W9-DHN-497

THE fun of making one's own goodies has been lost to many of the snackers of today. People used to have taffy pulls and corn popping sessions—more for the fun of it than for the food. Cooking up snacks can still be the best part of the party! And, as Floss Dworkin says, "Even if store-bought treats were cheaper, or as tasty, would they fill our place with such an aroma?"

OPEN this book to any section and you will find imaginative, tempting recipes, perhaps for foods you've always thought you'd like to try making yourself. Here is your chance. It's fun, it's easy, and it's rewarding. Try any of these recipes and you will surely agree that THE GOOD GOODIES are the best!

THE GOOD GOODIES

All Natural Recipes
for Snacks and Sweets

Stan and Floss Dworkin

FAWCETT CREST • NEW YORK

Copyright © 1974 by Stan and Floss Dworkin

Published by Fawcett Crest Books, a unit of CBS Publications, the Educational and Professional Publishing Division of CBS, Inc. by arrangement with Rodale Press, Inc.

All rights reserved. Distributed in the United States by Ballantine Books, a division of Random House, Inc., New York, and in Canada by Random House of Canada, Limited, Toronto, Canada.

ISBN 0-449-20222-4

Printed in the United States of America

First Fawcett Crest Edition: May 1979
10 9 8 7 6 5

Contents

Preface

What is a "good goody"?

Well, a "goody," as anyone can tell you (just walk up to strangers on the street), is a treat, a candy, a snack—anything that delights the taste buds.

A "*good* goody" is a treat that not only delights, but is good for you, too.

The message of *The Good Goodies* is that you can have both delightful taste *and* good nutrition.

You can have alternatives to the heavily-greased, heavily-sugared, heavily-salted, chemicaled, preserved, dyed commercial treats on the market.

And you needn't have guilt.

With these goodies you can permit your family and yourself treats without feeling you're doing something wrong.

We know about guilt. We spent years down that road, but we came back. We're still "addicted" to ice cream, but now it's our own—and a good food instead of a baddy.

You can come back, too—back to something more natural, more honest, more nutritious, and just as delicious as any treats you've ever had.

Welcome, pilgrim.

1

Ice Cream, Ice Milk, and Ices

The ice cream you buy is a Standard of Identity food. It may contain any of literally hundreds of chemical products, without listing them on the label. We suppose that it is possible to buy wholesome ice cream. Just barely possible. But until the ice cream makers are required by law to put their ingredients on their labels, you just can't be certain.

It is most likely that the ice cream you get in your supermarket is made with a collection of chemical fillers, texturizers, flavorings, colorings, and other artificial ingredients.

Why this chemical stew instead of the cream, sugar, and fruit that ice cream was originally? Chemicals are cheaper than cream and fruit; they can make an ice cream thick and creamy with a minimum of cream; they extend the shelf life, brighten the colors, and heighten the flavors.

So, when we have ice cream, it's ice cream we've made ourselves. We make it in an electric-powered ice cream maker (called a "freezer," even though it won't freeze the ice cream hard) that behaves in just the same way that a hand-cranked machine does.

And we seldom use cream.

Cream contains a lot of butterfat (in fact, pure cream is pretty much pure butterfat), and butterfat sits heavy on hardening arteries. Instead, we use powdered skim milk in our recipes (we haven't been able to make the recipes work with whole milk), using large amounts of the powder, which boosts the protein content of our ice creams enormously (while reducing the calories substantially as compared with cream).

And we never use sugar.

Sugar is the one ingredient you can be fairly sure is in your commercial ice creams, and sugar is really a "bad baddy." This processed sugar uses up B vitamins from your system, gives you cavities, and is a real villain in heart disease. A triple threat.

We use honey or maple syrup. For the stories on these more natural sweeteners, see "Ingredients" chapter.

Making Ice Cream

Our first happy experience with homemade ice cream was in the Pennsylvania Dutch country of Lancaster County, Pennsylvania. Mennonite friends of ours brought out their hand-cranker, and the men took turns cranking their arms off.

When we looked for a machine to buy, we first tried to get a hand-cranker but they are getting rare, besides, we were planning to try about 40 different recipes so it just didn't seem practical. So, the recipes that follow were standardized on an electric-powered ice cream machine, but they will do fine (but take longer) in your hand-cranker.

By the way, a recipe and instruction booklet came with the machine. We chose a simple-looking recipe, followed instructions, *and failed utterly*. Rather than return the machine immediately, though, we spoke to someone who had an electric machine and had made ice cream at home with it. His instructions bore little relationship to our pamphlet. We tried his way, and as you'd guess, it worked fine.

Conclusion: it's better to have someone who has made ice cream successfully tell you how he did it than to have all the wrong manufacturers' instruction booklets in the world.

Nomenclature

Read this: it's important. We use certain words and phrases in this chapter which may be confusing, so let's straighten them out now.

"Chilling" refers to putting the canister of the ice cream machine (full of the soft, unworked, milky mixture) in the refrigerator to cool, before freezing.

"Freezing" and "working" refer to the mixture going around in the ice cream machine or ice cream maker. As we'll explain later on, the machine gives you ice cream the texture of soft or custard ice cream, which must then be hardened.

"Hardening" refers to the change from a soft to a hard ice cream, and we usually harden our ice cream in the freezing compartment of our refrigerator.

Bubbles

It's not just the low temperature that freezes your ice cream: the air bubbles you beat into it have a lot to do with freezing. If you see a recipe for machine-made ice cream without beating at some stage or another, be wary.

The bubbles you beat into the mixture before it goes into the machine divide the mixture into smaller bits. These smaller bits freeze much faster than big bits. And so, bubbles are important.

Fruit in Ice Cream

If you are using fruit in your ice cream, make sure that your fruit is either chopped up small or that it goes into the mixture late-on. If you put large chunks of fruit into the mixture when it first goes into the machine, all the chunks will gather around the paddle and not get distributed. Even small chunks will tend to gather somewhat on the paddle.

Can You Use Ice Cubes?

Yes, but you have to crush them with a hammer or
something before you use them. You need better contact
(of ice with the container) than you can get with the
chunky cubes.

If you have an ice crusher, more power to you. Or
you could buy crushed ice, we suppose. At any rate, the
ice should be in smallish bits.

But we've never been able to make enough cubes in
our own freezing compartment for a batch of ice cream.
(We don't have much trouble borrowing ice cubes from
the neighbors: we repay them with ice cream.)

Salt

All the recipes for machine-made ice cream call for
rock salt—which we never see in New York City except
in the winter. In case you've wondered, the salt lowers
the temperature of the ice water. Without it, your ice
cream is unlikely to freeze. We use coarse salt (kosher-
ing salt) but any salt will do. A 3-pound box makes about
3 batches of ice cream. We don't measure it: we just pour
a good helping over the ice every time we put in a layer
of ice.

Chilling Is Very Important

To chill, you place your made-up mixture, in the
canister, into the refrigerator (not in the freezer). If you
have a super fridge, then 2 hours chilling may be enough;
if you have an antique like ours, you'll need more like 4
hours. Don't skimp on the chilling. A well-chilled mixture
may make up in ½ hour, while one not well chilled may
require 2 hours of churning in the machine before it begins to freeze. This constitutes a real saving in electricity.

Icing and Salting

After you've chilled the canister, set it into the outside
bucket of your ice cream maker. Put a layer of crushed

ice about 2 inches deep into the bottom of the bucket. Pour or spoon on a good layer of salt (not thick, but a layer that covers most of the ice in sight), more ice, then more salt. Keep on with this layering until the ice comes up *higher than the canister*. This will work down very soon after you turn on the machine. As you go along, more ice and salt will have to be added, to keep the level of the ice higher than the ice cream. So, don't think that first layering is all the ice you're going to need.

When Is It Done?

If you're making a large recipe, the motor of your machine may labor, and that can be a sign that the ice cream is getting done.

Or, if your canister has a transparent top, you'll be able to see what's going on inside. It's very interesting. As the ice cream mixture gets harder and harder, it tends to climb up the paddles. As it hardens further, you can see the lines made by the paddles begin to hold rather than melt back into the whole. But, really, the only way to tell if your ice cream is hard enough to take out of the machine is to spoon out a bit and see. *Ice cream won't get as hard as commercial kinds here in the machine.* It is done with the machine when it reaches the texture of a frozen custard. (If you like frozen custard, you can eat it immediately.)

The half-hard ice cream can be left in the machine to harden: plug the drainage hole; cover the canister with ice; and top everything with a large piece of burlap.

Or, you can spoon the half-hard ice cream into covered containers and put them into your refrigerator's freezer to harden.

We prefer the latter because we never have enough ice for the burlap bit, and it gets messy to deal with that much melted ice and salt.

We will give you a machine-working time with every recipe, but these will really depend on how well you've chilled.

Getting It Out

When you stop the machine, the ice cream canister will be surrounded by a mixture of salt and ice. And there is nothing good goody about salty ice cream. So be careful. Wipe off the top and sides before you open the canister. Wrap a clean towel around the canister as you spoon out the ice cream (into containers with covers) in order not to let any of that salty mixture get in.

Saving the Ice

Now, this may sound strange, but if you have to borrow ice cubes to make ice cream, you can save the ice from making to making, and here's how.

First of all, drain the free water out of the bucket. (Hold a large strainer over the edge and tilt. Try not to use your hand as a strainer: this salty ice is *cold*.) Then, hold a large and sturdy plastic bag at the bucket's edge, and pour the unmelted ice into the bag. Tie it off with a twist tie, and put it into your freezer. This ice keeps very well for quite a while. And it will need supplementing by only 3 or 4 more trays when you make a new batch of ice cream.

Interchangeability

Strange as it seems, *instant* and *noninstant* powdered skim milks are *interchangeable* in the recipes that use powdered milk. Yes—if a recipe calls for 1 cup of *instant*, you may substitute 1 cup of *noninstant*, and *vice versa*. (The recipes with noninstant are much higher in protein.)

Without a Machine

You can make an ice cream of sorts without a freezing machine, provided your ice-cube trays have removable dividers.

Mix up a small ice-milk recipe, and distribute it among your ice-cube trays, filling each between half and three-quarters full. Put them into your freezer, and allow ice milk to begin to freeze. Remove trays from the freezer, and with a fork, stir ice milk well. Return to the freezer and allow to harden somewhat again, then stir with a fork again. Repeat until the ice cream is as hard as you want it.

Be warned that with this method, the ice cream often comes out full of ice crystals.

MAPLE ICE CREAM

This is the only true ice cream in the book, and we recommend it only for very active and underweight kids and adults. (The other recipes are not made with cream, but with super-rich powdered milk.) It is truly delicious.

1 cup maple syrup	*1 egg white (See "Cakes"*
4 large egg yolks	*chapter for "Separating*
1 pint heavy cream	*Eggs.")*

Measure the syrup into a saucepan and bring it to a bare simmer over low heat.

Heat water in the bottom of a double boiler to a simmer.

Meanwhile, put the egg yolks into the top of the double boiler (which is not yet over heat). Whisk them until well beaten.

Very slowly, and beating all the time, drip the heated syrup into the yolks. When well beaten, put the top onto the bottom of the double boiler, and stir egg mixture with a spoon until it is thick enough to coat the spoon: about 10 to 15 minutes.

Whip the cream in a large bowl until it is half stiff.

Add the egg white to the cream and beat stiff.

Cool the egg-and-syrup mixture. (We do this by filling the bottom of the double boiler with cold water, stirring the mixture in the top, and then replacing the water as it warms.)

When cool, dribble it into the whipped cream, beating all the while.

When mixed well, pour into the ice cream machine's canister, put in the paddle, cover, and chill for 3 to 4 hours.

When chilled, work in the ice cream maker as described in the beginning of this chapter, for about 45 minutes.

Harden ice cream in your freezer or deep freeze until you get the texture you like.

Yield: about 1½ quarts

MAPLE ICE MILK

The moment of truth. Is this recipe (and those that follow), made with powdered milk, as tasty and creamy as the same recipe would be made with cream? Yes, pretty much. And virtually no butterfat, plus additional lecithin to help break down cholesterol. In fact, we found the all-cream homemade ice cream rather too rich for our taste. (Most commercial ice creams are made without much cream, anyhow, and that's where most of us get our taste for "ice cream.")

It is harder to whip powdered milk into a stiff mixture than it is to whip cream. Cream beats and hold stiff, while, for us, the powdered milk never gets to that same "stiff peak" stage. See *Whipped Topping* in the "Miscellany" chapter, for details, though we will give you some reminders here.

You *must* use ice water: not cold tap water, but ice water.

You *must* chill your beaters and your bowl (just stick them in the fridge for about 15 minutes). If you don't, you could find yourself whipping all day without getting anything whipped.

With a rubber spatula, reach carefully into the bowl from time to time and stir the thinner outside stuff back into the thicker middle. That helps.

And be patient. It can take as long as *20 minutes* to beat the milk mixture into something stiff enough to use.

Don't omit the lecithin granules (see "Ingredients" chapter). They are easy to find in most health food stores, and they do help to make a really creamy dessert. Also, they do a number on cholesterol.

1 cup maple syrup	1/4 cup lecithin granules
4 large egg yolks (See "Cakes" chapter for "Separating Eggs.")	4 large egg whites
	1 cup instant milk powder
	1 cup ice water

Put large mixing bowl and beaters into refrigerator to cool for 15 minutes.

In a saucepan, bring the maple syrup to a bare simmer.

Put water in the bottom of a double boiler and heat to a simmer.

In the top of the double boiler, off the stove, beat the egg yolks until frothy.

Remove the syrup from the heat and very slowly, beating all the while, drip the syrup into the yolks.

Put the top of the double boiler over the simmering bottom; cook for 5 minutes, stirring frequently.

Add the lecithin granules and continue to cook, stirring frequently, until the mixture thickens, 10 to 15 minutes more.

Cool this mixture by setting the top of the double boiler in cold water.

In a large chilled bowl, beat the whites until they are half stiff.

Add the milk powder and ice water, and beat until quite stiff, about 10 minutes, stirring the thinner outside into the thicker inside occasionally.

When the maple mixture is cooled, add it gradually to the whipped milk and whites, and beat in well.

Scrape into the ice cream freezer canister and chill in your fridge for 3 to 4 hours.

Make in the ice cream machine, as described in the beginning of this chapter, for about 45 minutes.

Spoon into covered containers and set in your freezer compartment or deep freeze to harden.

Yield: about 1½ quarts
  (besides what you lick off the paddle)

MAPLE WALNUT ICE MILK

While the previous recipe was made with *instant* milk powder, this recipe is made with *noninstant* milk powder. Though less powder is used, by volume, we still increase the milk protein by more than 50 percent. By volume noninstant has more than twice the protein of instant.

Remember, add the nut chunks only after the ice cream has worked until it is almost ready to go into your refrigerator's freezer.

1 cup maple syrup	*1 cup ice water*
2 large egg yolks (See	*¾ cup noninstant milk*
"Cakes" chapter for	*powder*
"Separating Eggs.")	*1 cup walnut nutmeats,*
¼ cup lecithin granules	*coarsely chopped*
2 large egg whites	

Put a large mixing bowl and your beaters into the refrigerator to chill.

Put water in bottom of a double boiler and bring to a boil.

Combine the maple syrup, yolks, and lecithin in the top of the double boiler.

Put top of boiler over bottom and cook over high heat for about 10 minutes, stirring frequently, until the lecithin dissolves.

Remove from the heat and cool by placing top of double boiler in a bowl of cold water.

In the chilled bowl, beat the egg whites until frothy. Add the water and milk powder, and beat for about 10 minutes or until quite stiff.

When the syrup mixture is cooled, drip it into the egg-and-milk mixture, beating all the while.

Scrape into the canister of the ice cream maker and chill in refrigerator for about 3 hours.

When thoroughly chilled, freeze, as described in the beginning of this chapter, for about ½ hour.

When fairly firm, add the walnut chunks and allow to mix in the machine for about 1 minute more.

Can the ice milk and harden it in your refrigerator's freezer or your deep freeze.

Yield: about 1 quart

RICH COFFEE ICE MILK

This makes a good dessert for an adult who has a coffee habit (and caffeine is habit forming). We wouldn't serve it to children, however. Kids don't need to get introduced to coffee, even in a decaffeinated or substitute form. There are lots of noncoffee-flavored desserts they can have.

As you see, we use 3 tablespoons of instant decaffeinated coffee (which is a lot), but you can use a coffee substitute if you prefer. Just be sure you don't use one that contains sugar. This amount of instant coffee would be enough to make 9 cups of beverage: use an equivalent amount of the substitute.

1 cup water	*¼ cup lecithin*
½ cup honey	*granules*
3 tablespoons instant decaf-	*4 large egg whites*
feinated coffee	*1 cup noninstant*
4 large egg yolks (See	*milk powder*
"Cakes" chapter for	*1 cup ice water*
"Separating Eggs.")	

Put a large mixing bowl and your beaters into the refrigerator to chill for 15 minutes.

Put water into the bottom of a double boiler and bring to a boil.

Mix the first five ingredients in the top of a double boiler.

Put top of boiler over bottom and cook over high heat, stirring frequently, for about 10 minutes or until the lecithin is dissolved.

Remove from heat and cool by placing top of double boiler in cold water.

In the chilled bowl, beat the egg whites until half stiff.

Add the milk powder and ice water and beat until quite stiff.

When the coffee mixture is cooled, add it to the beaten fluff and beat in.

Scrape into the ice cream machine's canister and chill in the refrigerator for 3 to 4 hours.

Make in the ice cream machine, as described in the beginning of this chapter, for ¾ to 1 hour.

Scrape into covered containers and harden in your freezer compartment or deep freeze.

Yield: about 1½ quarts

Fruit Ice Milks

Fruit ice milks are lovely, in or out of season. In season we use fresh fruits. But, out of season, we use unsweetened, frozen organic fruits. These make up into ice cream much faster than the fresh fruits. Since we use the fruit still frozen, the cold fruit chills the mixture, and there's no need for the usual chilling in the refrigerator.

STRAWBERRY ICE MILK

To make this recipe with fresh berries, follow all the steps described, but then chill for 3 to 4 hours before freezing in your ice cream maker.

The ¾ cup of honey given below is very much a "to taste" measure. Taste the strawberry and honey mixture. If it is too tart, you may want to add some more honey, but keep in mind that everything is going to be diluted when you add it to the whipped "cream."

But you must decide now, before you put the ice milk up to freeze. Don't add honey to the canister; it will likely not mix, but collect on the paddles or around the sides. Honey hardens when it gets cold.

You'll notice we use no eggs in this recipe: this means it will be more difficult to whip the milk powder stiff.

¾ cup ice water	1 quart frozen straw-
¾ cup noninstant milk	berries (1¼ pounds)
powder	¾ cup honey
1 teaspoon vanilla extract	

Put a large mixing bowl and beaters into the fridge for about 30 minutes to chill well.

In the chilled bowl, make up the ice water and milk powder, beating until stiff (perhaps as much as 20 minutes).

When almost stiff, add the vanilla extract.

In a blender, process together the honey and berries, until you have a very thick purée. Taste for more honey.

Scrape into the beaten "cream" and beat in well.

No chilling period is required if you've used hard-frozen fruit. Put mixture directly into the canister of your ice cream maker and make for about ¾ hour, or until set, as described at the beginning of this chapter.

Spoon into covered containers and put into your freezer compartment or deep freeze to harden.

Yield: about ½ gallon

PAPAYA ICE MILK

It may not be easy for you to find unsweetened and organically-grown frozen papaya, but it certainly is worth the search. Village Market Foods packages one.

¾	cup noninstant milk powder	1¼	pounds frozen papaya
¾	cup ice water	¾	cup honey to
1	teaspoon vanilla extract		taste

Proceed as with *Strawberry Ice Milk*, above.

Yield: about ½ gallon

RICH CHERRY ICE MILK

Pie cherries are tart, but they have superior flavor, so, don't substitute bing cherries.

We use frozen cherries from an organic source. We pit the cherries while they are still frozen. They're terribly cold, but otherwise easier to handle. We take a knife (it doesn't have to be sharp and shouldn't be serrated) and cut down into the cherry, pressing hard for an instant against the stone. This loosens the stone, and when you open the cherry, the stone can just be flicked out.

You *will* have to chill this recipe, since you cook the cherries.

1¼	pounds frozen pie cherries, weighed with pits in	1	cup honey
		2	large egg whites
2	large egg yolks (See "Cakes" chapter for "Separating Eggs.")	¾	cup noninstant milk powder
		¾	cup ice water
⅓	cup lecithin granules	½	teaspoon almond extract

Set a large mixing bowl and beaters into the fridge to chill for about 15 minutes.

Pit the cherries and put them, along with the egg yolks, lecithin, and honey into your blender container and process at low speed until you have a chunky purée.

Boil water in the bottom of a double boiler.

Pour cherry mixture into the top of the double boiler and put boiler top over bottom. Cook 10 to 15 minutes, until the lecithin dissolves, stirring frequently. Remove from the heat and cool by setting the top of the double boiler into cold water.

In the chilled mixing bowl, beat the whites until half stiff.

Add the milk powder, ice water, and almond extract, and beat stiff.

When the cherry mixture is cooled, beat it into the whipped milk and egg whites.

Scrape into the ice cream machine's canister, and chill the canister for about 3 hours.

Make in the ice cream machine for 35 to 45 minutes, as described at the beginning of this chapter.

Spoon into covered containers and set in your freezer compartment or deep freeze to harden.

Yield: about ½ gallon

TART CHERRY ICE MILK

Here's a recipe that comes out much lighter than the egg ice milks. Pit the cherries as described in *Rich Cherry Ice Milk* (see above).

This recipe is really tart. If you don't like it tart, add more honey to the blended cherries.

¾ cup ice water	1¼ pounds frozen pie
¾ cup noninstant milk	cherries (1 quart)
powder	½ cup honey (or more
½ teaspoon almond extract	to taste)

Make up as described for *Strawberry Ice Milk* (see above).

When the cherries are pureed, taste for more honey.

There is no need to chill. Make in your ice cream maker for 35 to 45 minutes as described at the beginning of this chapter.

When set, scrape into covered containers and put into your freezer compartment or deep freeze to harden.

Yield: about ½ gallon

BANANA ICE MILK

Bananas seem to make things richer than they are. This recipe comes out quite creamy, without cream or eggs or lecithin.

Make sure the bananas you use are soft and strong-smelling, not firm and half green. Only the really ripe ones give you that great banana flavor.

¾ cup noninstant milk powder	1 teaspoon vanilla extract
¾ cup ice water	3 medium bananas, peeled
	¾ cup honey

Put a large mixing bowl and beaters into the refrigerator to chill for 30 minutes.

Then measure the milk powder and ice water into the chilled bowl and beat until quite stiff: about 20 minutes.

Measure the remaining ingredients into your blender and process into a mush.

Scrape the banana mixture into the whipped milk and beat until smooth.

Scrape into the canister of your ice cream maker and chill in the refrigerator for 3 to 4 hours.

Make in the ice cream machine, as described earlier in this chapter, about 45 minutes.

Spoon into covered containers and set in your deep freeze or freezer compartment to harden.

Yield: about 1½ quarts

ICES

In *Blend It Splendid* we did a whole section on making *Ices* in your blender. We'll include only these two recipes here, but it's really simple to invent your own. What you need is ½ cup of liquid (liquefied fruit, or sweetener plus fruit, for instance), and about 1 large tray of ice cubes.

Put the liquid into the blender container (or process the fruit), then add a few ice cubes. With the machine set for high speed, turn it on and off, until the cubes are mostly chopped. Add more cubes, and continue in the same way. You should reach a point when you won't have to turn on and off, when the machine will grind the cubes continuously. Keep adding cubes until the *Ice* is as thick as you want it. Spoon out to serve immediately or allow to harden for a few hours in your freezer compartment.

LO-CAL MOCHA ICE

Here is an ice that comes out refreshing and tasty without being sweet.

3 *heaping teaspoons carob powder*	3 *heaping teaspoons non-instant milk powder*
2 *heaping teaspoons coffee substitute*	¼ *cup cold water* ⁣*ice cubes*

Measure the dry ingredients into the blender, then add the water and mix briefly.

Add the cubes and process as described in "Ices" (above).

Yield: about 4 servings

PINEAPPLE ICE

Pineapple does not blend up very liquid—even with a few tablespoons of honey added, it is still half solid.

You can make the same kind of ice with cantaloupe or watermelon—or any yellow or orange melon (all are rich in vitamin A).

Six ounces of pineapple is one slice of a large pineapple, about ½-inch thick. A kitchen scale makes it simpler to measure.

The amount of honey you need will vary according to the sweetness of your pineapple.

6 *ounces fresh pineapple*	1 to 1¼ *trays*
3 *tablespoons honey*	*ice cubes*

Cut the pineapple into chunks, put in the blender container with the honey, and blend until it is a thick liquid.

Taste for more honey.

Add a few cubes and blend at high speed until half crushed. (You may have to do a lot of poking with your spatula to get the cubes to the blades, but SHUT THE MACHINE OFF WHEN YOU POKE.)

Keep adding cubes until the mixture is very thick.

Yield: 4 small servings

2

Jams, Jellies, and Preserves

We used to buy commercial jams, before we learned the truth about processed sugars.

Then we went to the health food stores, to buy honey jams, but were shocked to find that the ones we saw had both honey *and* sugar. For a long while after that we just didn't eat any jams at all.

After all, they are not essential to human nutrition. But every so often we had a longing for something sweet with our breakfast toast or with our homemade whole wheat English muffins. So we decided to make our own jams.

Yes: jams, jellies, preserves, marmalades and conserves, all can be made successfully with honey and fruit, and nothing else. None of the chemicals and manufactured sweeteners that the FDA allows to go unlabeled on Standard of Identity foods are necessary.

Make no mistake about it, most of these spreads are quite high in calories. But, we have to add that these honey jams, honey jellies, and honey preserves are much better tasting than any comparable product you can buy. And far superior to even homemade jams made with sugar.

When the editor of this book, Charles Gerras, asked us if honey didn't mask the flavor of the fruit in a jam, our answer was to take out a sample of *Orange Marmalade* we had brought for him and let him taste for himself. No, honey does not mask the flavor. It enhances the flavor.

Did your family make jam when you were a child? We don't ask, "Did your mother make jam?" because it wasn't just mother, but aunts and neighbors, too, all working in a steaming kitchen for a whole day and into the night. Our Mennonite friends still do it that way. But that isn't for us.

More to our style is a *Cranberry Jelly* which requires only five minutes cooking. Even our slower recipes don't really have to be tended until the final few minutes of cooking.

These jams keep well. The honey in them acts as a preservative, discouraging molds. The smaller the amount of honey, the more likely that mold will eventually form. To be on the safe side, we refrigerate our jams. We did leave out a jar of *Peach Jam*, and a jar of Floss's favorite, *Tomato Jam*. The *Peach* formed a bit of mold after about two weeks, so we refrigerated it and no more mold formed. The *Tomato* showed no sign of mold after two months. Still, these are foods without chemical preservatives, and it's best to refrigerate them. In the refrigerator, they keep for months and months.

The recipes are simple, with few ingredients. Some people feel that a recipe can't be really good unless it has many ingredients (and a few French verbs). Don't you believe it. These recipes require no skill or special equipment. They are all made on top of the stove, in a saucepan, and stirred with a spoon or rubber spatula.

No additional pectin is added. Not that there's anything wrong with pectin—many fruits have pectin in them naturally. Apples, cranberries, beach plums, and other fruits have it. There is even a commercial pectin made from apples. You can also buy commercial jellers whose labels read like chemical soups. But the point is that you just don't need them. Our jams and jellies thicken on their own, without help. Some from their own pectin, some from the thickening of the cooked honey.

Honey is a liquid because of the water it contains. When it was nectar in the flowers, it was much more liquid. The bees in their hives cause much of the liquid to evaporate, by vibrating their wings and creating air currents. When it is the right consistency, the bees seal the honey cells with wax. You can thicken honey or even make it solid by just simmering off enough water (for instructions see chapter on "Cooked Candies"). Similarly, when you simmer a jam, you boil off water from the honey and it thickens.

All of these recipes are for small amounts. The biggest *(Grapefruit Jam)* yields only about 2½ cups, while the smallest *(Tomato Jam)* yields less than one cup.

There are several reason for this. We don't like to make large amounts of any sweet. It is too tempting. With these small recipes, your wickedness is limited.

We don't have a farm (unless you count our tiny balcony with miniature tomato plants on it as a farm), and we live in the city without a car, so large amounts of fruit are very seldom available to us.

And, making large amount of jams means large investments of time and we're unwilling to make that investment. Doubling any of these recipes will almost double the cooking time.

We try to make jams out of whatever fruit (like tomatoes) is cheap and in good supply. If we can get a very good buy on a large amount of fruit, we'll make a butter instead of a jam. Butters require less honey, and less cooking time in proportion to the amount of fruit.

Use unsprayed fruit whenever possible. The insecticides used by most commercial growers don't wash off the skins easily, and the skins are used in most of the following recipes. Why not avoid these poisons if you can? Shop around: in season, organically-grown fruits are often cheaply available from local farmers.

Warning

Honey scorches, so it must be cooked over a flame just high enough to simmer it. These recipes call for low flames, and that means *simmering low*. This slows the cooking, but it ensures you against scorching, and keeps the color of the finished jam close to the color of the fresh fruit.

Jarring

For people like us, getting jars can be a problem. Certain of the special honeys we like come in small jars, and we recycle these for years and years. But we don't buy mayonnaise, and we don't use instant coffee, or buy peanut butter, and so getting jars is no simple matter.

If you are in the same boat, you may be forced to buy small canning jars. Or maybe you can get small jars from your recycling center.

It is not necessary to sterilize your jars: just wash them very well—including the tops.

We jar our jams as soon as they are cool enough to spoon in without cracking the glass, then we refrigerate them while they are still hot. Nothing special, nothing difficult.

CRANBERRY JELLY

If you've never made a jelly before in your life, start here. Follow the instructions, and you can't fail.

This recipe cooks in five minutes. The cranberries have so much pectin in them that the honey needn't go through long cooking to thicken the jelly. In fact, pectin has the property of *losing* its jelling power if you cook it too long, so don't feel that if five minutes is good, 15 minutes is even better. It's not.

Fresh cranberries have a very short season and we would never buy canned. But we've found that we can keep cranberries frozen for several months, even in our refrigerator's lousy freezer section, and they still keep their flavor and texture. The day after the holiday season, our fruit man reduces the cranberry price, so we buy several extra pounds and freeze them uncooked. *After* the holidays is the cheapest time to make *Cranberry Jelly*.

1 pound cranberries   *1 cup honey*

Wash the cranberries well and pick over to remove any stems or bad berries, then put cranberries into a 2- or 3-quart pot, with enough hot water to cover.

Bring to a boil and continue to boil, covered (the cranberries pop), for 5 minutes.

Remove from the heat, drain off the cranberry water (you can reserve it for a cranberry cocktail), and press the berries with a slotted spoon to remove more water.

Spoon the berries into a quart jar.

Add the honey to the jar and stir thoroughly until the honey is completely distributed.

Place in the refrigerator to cool and set. No further jelling aid is needed.

Serve as a jelly or as a cranberry sauce.

Yield: about 3 cups

QUICK LEMON MARMALADE

Part of the success of this recipe comes from really slivering the lemons. Use a very sharp knife. But first, be certain you scrub the lemons clean. They may not be dyed, but they are probably sprayed. And watch out for the ink the produce man uses to stamp on the price. If you can't scrub the price off, just cut it off.

1 cup honey   *3 medium-sized lemons*

In a 3-quart pot, bring honey to a boil over a low flame, and simmer it, uncovered, for about 8 minutes.

Meanwhile, scrub, pit, and sliver the lemons. Add lemons to the honey (peel, pulp, and all) and simmer, to thicken, uncovered, for 20 to 25 minutes, stirring frequently toward the end of the cooking.

It should be a bit thinner than the texture you want for marmalade, when you remove it from the heat. It will thicken further as it cools.

This marmalade winds up nice and chewy (be careful, the thicker you make the slivers, the chewier it gets).

Yield: about 1 cup

PLUM JAM

The last time we made this jam we used President plums, but any variety will do. In season, the Italian plums (prunes) are plentiful and relatively inexpensive.

If the plums are not sweet, you may want to increase the honey to ¾ cup.

1 pound fresh plums	⅝ cup honey
(weighed with pits)	¼ teaspoon cinnamon

Wash the plums well, pit them, and cut in halves. Put into a large pot.

Add the honey and stir.

Simmer, uncovered, about 40 minutes over a very low heat, stirring often.

During the last few minutes of cooking, add the cinnamon.

Yield: about 1¼ cups

WILD BLUEBERRY JAM

Wild blueberries have a stronger, more tart flavor than the usual domestic varieties. They are also smaller and, perhaps best of all, these wild berries are available frozen all year round (they are at our health food co-op).

The combination of tart fruit and sweet honey really makes elegant tasting jams.

2 cups wild blueberries	grated rind of 1 small
¾ cup honey	lemon

Combine all the ingredients in a 3- or 4-quart pot and simmer, uncovered, over a very low flame for about 40 to 45 minutes, stirring frequently, especially during the final stages of cooking.

Remove from the heat when thickish.

Yield: more than 1 cup

TOMATO JAM

We had never tasted, or seen a recipe for, *Tomato Jam* until we made this one. So we don't know how the flavor compares with other tomato jams, but we do know it is incredibly delicious—the best jam we ever tasted.

½ cup honey	1 teaspoon basil
1 pound tomatoes	salt (to taste)
¼ teaspoon ground cloves	

In a 3- to 4-quart pot, simmer the honey over a very low flame for 5 minutes.

Wash and trim the tomatoes, but don't peel them.

Cut an opening in each, and squeeze over a bowl to remove much of the seeds and juice. (Set this juice aside or drink it now—it doesn't go into the recipe.)

Cut the tomatoes into small pieces and add them, along with the cloves and basil, to the honey.

Cook, uncovered, for about 40 minutes, or until thick. Toward the end of cooking, taste for a possible dash or two of salt.

Yield: more than ¾ cup

PINEAPPLE PRESERVES

We think of preserves as having more chunks of fruit than jams have. The definition is an arbitrary one, but this recipe is excellent for those of us who like to chew our jam.

Don't use canned pineapple (see *Pineapple Muffins*, page 87, for why).

From one large pineapple, we made this jam, a batch of *Pineapple Muffins*, and had a bit to eat fresh.

1 pound fresh pineapple meat (trimmed)	1 cup honey

Cut the pineapple into small chunks (but do not grind), saving as much of the juice as you can. Dump chunks and juice into a 3-quart pot.

Add the honey, stir, and cook, uncovered, for about 1¼ hours over very low heat, stirring occasionally (stir more frequently as the mixture thickens).

Yield: about 2 cups

PEACH JAM

The amount of honey you really need for *Peach Jam* depends on the season and the natural sweetness of the peaches. Taste them before you cook. If they are very early (or very late in the season) you may want to add a couple of tablespoons of honey. You can wait until the jam is half-cooked before deciding.

*1 pound peaches (weighed   ¼ cup honey
   with pits)*

Scrub, pit, but do not peel, the peaches. Cut them into small chunks and put into a 3-quart pot.

Add the honey and stir.

Cook uncovered over simmering low heat for about 45 minutes or until thick, stirring occasionally (but more frequently as the jam thickens).

Yield: about 1 cup

ORANGE MARMALADE

The white rind (between the outer skin of an orange and the tough shell around the pulp) contains bioflavonoids which good nutritionists say have an important place in nutrition. Ordinarily you should eat as much of this rind as you can leave on the orange. Unfortunately, it cooks up very tough in a marmalade, and, if you leave patches of it on the chunks of orange, you get tough white patches of it in the marmalade. So, peel off as much as you can.

We like to use a combination of oranges for this recipe: temples, navels, juice oranges—whatever is available. But we prefer navels for their peel which has a good texture and flavor.

2 pounds oranges (weighed with skins on)	3/4 cup honey rind of 1 navel orange

Peel the oranges, pit them, and cut up into small chunks. Put them all in a large pot.

Add the honey.

Shave the navel orange peel into fine slices and add.

Stir and cook, uncovered, over a simmering-low flame for about 40 minutes or until thick.

Yield: about 1½ cups

GRAPEFRUIT JAM

With grapefruit, leaving on any of the white middle rind makes for a bitterness no amount of honey can cover. So, after you've peeled your grapefruit, take a knife and get as much of that white off as you possibly can. The success of the recipe depends upon it.

3 large grapefruits (about 3 pounds total weight)	1 cup honey

Peel, pit, and chunk the grapefruit, and put it into a large pot.

Add the honey and stir.

Cook, uncovered, over simmering-low heat for 1½ hours or until thick, stirring occasionally early on, then more frequently as the cooking progresses.

Yield: 2½ cups

APPLE CONSERVE

Yes, you can get jellies out of apples, too. In fact, tart apples have a lot of natural pectin. This conserve is thicker than most jellies and, when it's finished cooking,

you can see only apple. You're boiling away all the
liquids in the honey, so do keep stirring or you'll scorch
this recipe.

1 pound apples   *½ cup honey*

Wash and core, but do not peel, the apples. Dice them
small and dump into a 3-quart pot.

Add the honey.

Simmer, uncovered, over the lowest flame about 20 minutes or until all the honey disappears.

Stir frequently. In the final minutes, stir constantly.

Yield: more than a cup

FIG JAM (No Honey)

Here's a jam made without any additional sweetener
at all—just the natural fruit sugars from the figs themselves.

Cut up the figs quite small. They come out a bit chunky
if you don't.

1 pound dried figs

Wash the figs well, trim off the hard stem-ends, and cut
the figs into eighths or smaller.

Put them in a large pot and cover with about 3 cups of
hot water. Allow to soak overnight.

Next day, simmer figs, uncovered, over a medium-low
flame until most of the liquid is cooked off, then reduce
the heat.

Cook, uncovered, stirring frequently, until all the free
liquid is gone and the mixture is thick.

Yield: about 1 cup

PEAR BUTTER

Fruit butters are fruits and spices, cooked until thick
and smooth. Most recipes we've seen call for a long cook-

ing time. We've managed to get this recipe down to 2½ hours which for us is still very long and no source of pride. But we are proud of the flavor, and proud that we can make a *Pear Butter* this good without using anything artificial.

4½-5	pounds pears	3	teaspoons cloves
½	cup fresh lemon juice	2	teaspoons cinnamon
1	cup honey	½	teaspoon nutmeg

Wash and core, but do not peel, the pears. Cut them into small chunks and put them into a large pot.

Add the remaining ingredients and stir well.

Cook, uncovered, over a medium-low flame, until most of the free liquid is gone and the mixture is thickened, then reduce the flame and cook, stirring frequently, until quite thick—about 2½ hours.

After about ½ hour of cooking, take a potato masher and mash the pears up in the pot. The masher also makes a good stirrer. Even with mashing, this cooking isn't quite enough to get rid of all the chunks. We like the bits, but if you don't, run the butter through a blender after it cools.

Yield: more than 1 quart

APPLE BUTTER

Here is a butter that cooks up in about 1 hour.

5	pounds apples	2	teaspoons cinnamon
1	cup wine vinegar	1	teaspoon cloves
1½	cups honey	1	whole lemon
¼	teaspoon salt		

Wash and core the apples, but do not peel them.

Cut them into small chunks and dump the chunks into a large pot.

Add the vinegar, honey, salt, cinnamon and cloves, and stir in.

Wash and pit the lemon. Leaving the skin on, either cut the lemon up very small, or liquefy it in your blender. Add to pot and stir in.

Cook, covered, for about 15 minutes at medium temperature, then uncover. After removing the cover, mash apple mixture well with a potato masher.

Cook for an additional 50 minutes at low temperature.

Stir frequently in the later stages of cooking.

The butter is done when it is thick and smooth.

Yield: about 2 quarts

3

Raw Candies

Candies Without Guilt

We make our candies with wholesome, natural ingredients —without emulsifiers, without conditioners, without artificial flavorings, without carcinogenic colorings, without salt, without granulated sugar, without chocolate, without preservatives, without chemicals, and without harmful ingredients of any kind.

Which doesn't mean that our candies are "low cal." In fact, many of the chemical "nonfoods" in commercial candies are lower in calories than the nuts, seeds, fruits, honey, maple syrup and molasses that we use.

But are calories the whole ball of wax? Calories *do count*, but they don't count for everything. They are important, but they are not the be-all and the end-all.

Every sensible person, except those few lucky ones who never do gain weight no matter what they eat, should be aware of the calorie value of his or her diet.

But, the way we see it, if a candy can be made as healthy as any other wholesome food, then the candy *is* food, not just something extra you tack on with a feeling of guilt, but a wholesome, natural, and satisfying food.

You don't need us to do a number here on sugar; it should have a health warning or a skull on its package. Or on so-called "raw" sugar, which is much more expensive and only two percent better. Or on brown sugar, which is just the same as granulated white sugar with a little molasses added. There have been best-sellers written on the danger of sugar as a cause of heart disease, and plenty written on it as a source of cavities, and a cause of vitamin deficiencies.

So, don't buy your sweets, make them. You'll find the recipes in this section great fun to do with the whole family.

In these uncooked recipes the amount of sweetener should be adjusted to your taste.

Honey Balls

Here is a basic candy form that can be varied so much that it's like one of those magazine articles that promises "Forty Fantastic Outfits from Two Bodystockings and a Can of Day-Glo Paint!"

These balls feature sunflower and sesame seeds, and seeds are very "good goodies" all by themselves. They are rich in vitamins and minerals, including iron and E and a few B's and PABA and potassium and magnesium— all hard to come by if one indulges in today's super-refined diet.

We always use sesame seeds with the hulls on. Once the seeds are hulled, the oils can go rancid very quickly. (It was a long time before we found out that what we didn't like about the taste of sesame seeds was that we were eating hulled seeds that had already begun to turn rancid.)

Sunflower seeds keep longer out of the shell than sesame seeds do. But they take an eternity to shell if you do it by hand. When you buy them shelled, do keep them in the refrigerator. Everything that's alive at all keeps better in the fridge once it's been removed from its natural protective shell: that includes ground whole grains, seeds, nuts, etc.

SUNFLOWER BALLS

Here's the basic recipe: just two ingredients, and easy

and quick to make up. Though you do have to be prepared to get a bit of honey on your hands.

Don't hesitate to double this recipe.

If you use a blender, let the machine work as little as possible: blender grinding builds up heat and heat destroys some of the vitamins.

1 cup sunflower seeds   *2 rounded tablespoons honey*

In your blender or grinder, grind the seeds down to a fine flour, and dump the seed flour into a bowl.

Drip in about 2 tablespoons of honey and, with a fork, work the honey into the ground seeds until you have a cohesive mass. If your seeds won't cohere, add a bit more honey, and work in well again.

When very well mixed, spoon out teaspoonfuls of the mixture and shape into balls between the palms of your hands. With this little honey, the outsides of the balls should not be really sticky, and they may be placed right onto a dish for serving.

Yield: about 20 1-inch balls

SUNFLOWER-RAISIN BALLS

This variation requires more work. If we were using more honey (as we will later on), we could use the raisins whole. As it is, with this little honey, and this much raisin, we need the additional stickiness that the cut raisins give us.

1 cup sunflower seeds	*½ cup seedless manukka*
2½ rounded tablespoons	*raisins*
honey	

Grind the seeds and add the honey as described in *Sunflower Balls* (above).

Measure out the raisins and scissor them in halves, right into the same bowl.

Stir very well until as uniform as you can manage, then spoon out teaspoonfuls of the mixture and shape between the palms of your hands. You may have to press a bit more firmly to get the balls to hold together, because of the raisins.

Yield: about 24 balls

TWO-SEED HONEY BALLS

This recipe requires a bit of doing: three bowls and more stickiness. But it makes an excellent company candy. This is sweeter than the previous two—though you can reduce the honey slightly to your taste.

You're actually making Balls of two flavors in this recipe: carob and plain.

2 cups hulled sunflower seeds	1 heaping tablespoon carob powder
6 to 7 tablespoons honey	⅜ cup unhulled sesame seeds
3 tablespoons raisins	

In a blender or in a grinder, grind the sunflower seeds into a flour, and dump them into a mixing bowl.

Drip in the honey, and mix very well.

Add the raisins (whole) and mix until you have a sticky, cohesive mass.

Into one small bowl or saucer, measure the carob powder.

Into another small bowl or saucer, measure the sesame seeds.

With a teaspoon and your clean hands, shape a lump of the honey-sunflower mixture into a ball about 1 inch across.

One at a time, roll half the balls in carob powder until covered, and set them on a piece of waxed paper.

One at a time, roll the remaining balls in the sesame seeds, and set them directly onto a dish for serving.

After about 15 minutes, the honey should soak through the carob: now roll the carobed balls in sesame seeds, also, and set out to serve.

Yield: about 36 balls

Note:

You can eat these at once, or they'll keep in a covered box for a couple of days. For longer storage, keep them in your refrigerator.

HONEY NUT BALLS

You can use almost any nut for this recipe. But almonds, walnuts or filberts are especially good.

The tablespoon of blackstrap isn't enough to give the candy a strong flavor, but enough to add an additional measure of minerals and iron, and trace elements. Blackstrap is richer in those than anything but liver.

2 *cups shelled nuts*	3 *tablespoons raisins*
5 *tablespoons honey*	1 *heaping tablespoon*
1 *tablespoon blackstrap*	*carob powder*
molasses	⅜ *cup unhulled*
	sesame seeds

In a blender or grinder, grind the nuts to a flour, and dump them into a mixing bowl.

Add the honey and molasses and mix very well.

Proceed as directed in *Two-Seed Honey Balls* recipe (see above).

Yield: about 36 balls

SUNFLOWER-DATE BALLS

Make certain the dates are moist, or else these balls are likely to just fall apart. Add the honey a tablespoon at a time and mix very well after each tablespoon. You may be able to get the balls to hold together with less honey than called for in this recipe.

1 *cup hulled sunflower*	1 *cup dates*
seeds	¼ *cup honey*

In a blender or grinder, grind the seeds down to a fine flour and pour into a mixing bowl.

Pit the dates and scissor them up small. Mix the dates and ground seeds together very well.

Add the honey and mix until well blended.

When mixed, pick out a bit and roll it into a 1-inch ball between your palms. Repeat until all mixture is used.

Yield: about 30 1-inch balls

CASHEW BALLS

Use only raw cashews, please. The roasted nuts lose a good deal of their vitamin content, and raw cashews are quite tasty (unlike raw peanuts, which many people find too green in flavor).

Don't grind these nuts in the blender. You want coarser chunks than a blender can provide. Use a spring-mounted nut chopper instead: you'll get lots of fine flour along with the coarser bits that are so good for texture.

1 cup raw cashews   *2 tablespoons honey*

Chop the nuts and put them in a bowl.

Add the honey and mix very well.

Pick up teaspoonfuls and roll them between the palms of your hands.

Yield: about 12 balls

Note:
These are stickier than most of the other recipes in this group.

STUFFED DATES

Stuffed dates are always impressive party fare, but the commercial kinds often seem to have been in the box too long.

For straight eating and for most recipes calling for dates, we recommend the moist California dates: we find their flavor and texture superior. For this recipe you can use the California or the imported, either moist or rather dry. So long as it doesn't fall apart, any date will do.

Currants are species of small grapes—and like grapes they dry to a sort of raisin. You can use raisins if you can't find dried currants, but the currant flavor is a bit stronger.

1 cup seedless dried
  currants

½ cup desiccated coconut
  shreds
2 to 3 dozen dates

Grind the currants in a Mouli grater, allowing the grindings to drop into a large bowl.

Add the coconut, and mix very well, until almost uniform.

Pit the dates by cutting them halfway through, down their length and removing the stones.

With your fingers, pick up a bit of the coconut-currant mixture (a rough ball about ½ inch across) and stuff it into the pitted date. Press the date partly closed again, around the mixture, and there you are.

Yield: 24 to 36

Note:

You can stuff the dates thick or thin, as you prefer, hence the variable yield.

FANCY STUFFED DATES

Here is a *Stuffed Date* for when you want to show off. It is sweeter and has the extra goodness of the seeds.

1 cup seedless raisins
⅓ cup hulled sunflower
  seeds
24 to 30 dates

¼ cup honey
1 cup unhulled sesame
  seeds

Grind the raisins in a Mouli grater and drop the grindings into a large mixing bowl.

Add the whole sunflower seeds and mix very well.

Pit the dates by slitting halfway through lengthwise, and removing the stones.

Stuff the mixture into the dates.

In a small pan, warm the honey (don't heat it too hot—
you just want to thin it a bit).

Measure the sesame seeds into a small bowl or saucer.

Dip the stuffed dates in the warmed honey, then roll them
in the sesame seeds.

Yield: 24 to 30

Variation:

For an even kickier textural difference, you might
want to cook the honey for about 8 minutes (over a very
low flame), allow the honey to cool enough to handle,
then dip the dates in it and roll the dates in the seeds.
The honey will half harden.

For more cooked honey candies, see next chapter.

MOCK CHOCOLATE CLUSTERS

The carob mixture in this recipe can also be the base
for a fine pudding, or, with a bit more milk powder, a
really chocolatey icing.

Did you see that italicized "*y*"? When the advertising
people want you to think a product contains something
wholesome instead of a chemical substitute, they add that
"y" to the end of the word, and they're in the clear:
"lemony" (tasting *like* lemon, but just a chemical flavoring): "creamy" (probably there isn't a drop of cream in
the whole factory); and many others—including "chocolatey."

Actually, one can live very well without chocolate—
especially children. Besides all the sugar in any chocolate
candy (chocolate itself is bitter), the oxalic acid in chocolate can hinder the absorption of calcium.

To us, this recipe comes very close to sweet chocolate,
but it does have a drawback. As the carob mixture dries
(over the course of a few days), its color lightens, and it
takes on a look similar to the look chocolate gets when it
is stale and flavorless. The carob is neither stale nor
flavorless—but the candies look pale. So, eat these as
soon after making as you can—certainly within two or

three days. The carob may still be a bit moist, but that is all to the good.

The butter helps delay this drying out, but you can leave it out of the recipe if butter bothers you.

The lecithin granules make for a very smooth coating ("creamy," in fact). The commercial candymakers often use lecithin as an emulsifier. For a discussion of lecithin, see the "Ingredients" chapter.

Now, don't ask what a recipe that goes into the oven is doing in "Raw Candies." That 10 to 15 minutes is just a drying time, to evaporate a bit of the liquid. You could get the same effect by leaving the tray in the open for several hours.

½ cup warm water
2 tablespoons sweet butter
⅓ cup noninstant milk powder
½ cup carob powder

2 rounded tablespoons lecithin granules
1 cup shelled peanuts, with papers
1 cup currants (or raisins)

In a blender, mix together the water, butter, milk powder, carob, and lecithin granules, briefly, until smooth.

Put the peanuts and currants into a large mixing bowl and pour the carob mixture over them. Mix very well, until all the nuts and currants are covered with the carob mixture.

Very lightly, grease a large baking sheet (see chapter on "Greasing without Grease"), and spoon out teaspoonfuls of the mixture in clumps. If bits break away, push them back to the main cluster.

Starting in a cold oven, bake clusters on a middle rack until the tops barely begin to dry, about 10 to 15 minutes at 300° (low temperature).

Remove, and put aside for a few hours, until clusters are dry enough to handle.

Yield: anywhere from 15 to 30 clusters, depending on the size of your spoon

4

Cooked Candies

We're very proud of these candies. We work with *only* honey, molasses, and maple sugar as sweeteners, and we have still been able to get those interesting textural effects that were thought to be the exclusive property of processed white sugar. At the same time we get wholesome candies that taste nothing at all like "health food" candies. You've got to try them to believe them.

We hope you'll work on these recipes and then go on to adapt your favorite old granulated-sugar recipes on your own, turning them from old "bad baddies" into new "good goodies."

Warnings

1. Boiled honey, maple syrup, or molasses, is *hot*, and holds its heat a very long time. This makes any of these sweeteners extremely dangerous to use around small children—even more dangerous than boiling water. Boiling water runs off the surface of skin it touches, boiling honey sticks to the skin, which means that the heat is held on even longer. So, BE CAREFUL in handling these.

2. Cook honey, maple syrup, or molasses over a *very low flame*. These sweets scorch very easily, and they often must be cooked quite a while to get the water out of them. Stir them from time to time. And cook them only

in enameled pots which distribute the heat evenly, without hotspots.

Pleasures

Now, after frightening the bejeezus out of you, let us say that these candies are wildly delicious. They range from softish caramels to hardest suckers, depending on the amount of cooking you give them. No child or sweet-toothed adult will ever say no to them.

Candy Thermometers

If you can stick the bottom 2 inches of your thermometer into the cooking candy, then you can get an accurate reading. With the small amounts we use in these recipes, a candy thermometer is useless and confusing.

So, rather than putting our trust in thermometers, we're going to describe ways of testing for candy doneness with honey, maple syrup, and molasses.

Candy Testing

Candy doneness is reported in terms of "soft ball," "medium ball," and "hard ball."

These terms describe the behavior of a drop of cooked syrup when it is dripped into a bowl of ice water (or at least very cold water). As the time approaches the cooking time indicated in the recipe, drip a bit of the hot syrup into a large bowl of very cold water.

If the syrup drifts toward the bottom and breaks up into tiny bits, it is too soft even to measure.

If the syrup stays cohesive on the bottom, reach in, pick it up, and squeeze it between your fingers (still in the bowl). If, as you squeeze, a cohesive but still easily flattened ball forms between your fingers, the syrup has reached the "soft-ball" stage.

If, when you squeeze it, the ball offers more resistance, you've reached the "medium-ball" stage.

Finally, if, when you squeeze it, the syrup forms into

a ball that gives little if at all, you've reached the "hard-ball" stage.

As a preliminary guide to when you are reaching a testable stage, you can dip a teaspoon into the cooking syrup and pull it out, coated with the syrup. Blow on it to cool, and see how thick and viscous, or even how hard, the coating on the spoon is. But this is only an indicator, not a real test.

GLAZED ALMONDS

Here's a cooked-honey recipe that's simple because the honey requires no additional handling. You just dip the almonds in, scoop them out, with a slotted spoon, and spread them to dry.

Should you find that (because you have not cooked it long enough) the honey won't harden, then, when they are cooled, roll the still-sticky almonds in desiccated coconut.

½ cup honey   *1 cup shelled almonds*

In a small saucepan, over very low (simmering-low) heat, boil the honey until it tests at "hard ball" (see the beginning of this chapter for "Candy Testing"), about 15 minutes. Allow the foam to settle.

Grease a dinner plate *very* lightly (see "Greasing without Grease" chapter).

Drop a handful of almonds into the hot honey, swish them around with a slotted spoon to make certain they are well covered, then scoop them out, allowing the excess honey to drip back into the pot.

Drop the coated almonds onto the plate and separate them with a clean knife. (You can leave a few in clumps, if you wish.)

Repeat until all the honey is used up. You may need more than one plate.

Allow the almonds to cool, and harden, then scrape them off the plate to serve. If the remaining honey hardens be-

fore you've finished all the almonds, reheat it gently for a
moment, until it becomes liquid again.

Yield: lots

OLD MAN ALMONDS

We call this recipe *Old Man Almonds* because the bit
of coconut shreds on the thick end look like nothing so
much as a head of white hair.

In this recipe, you're going to have to dip each almond
by hand into the hot honey. So do be careful.

If you prefer, you can use a pair of tongs to hold one
nut at a time.

½ cup honey   1 cup almonds,
½ cup desiccated coconut   shelled
   shreds

In a small saucepan, bring the honey to a boil over very
low heat and allow to simmer for about 8 minutes (no
need to stir if the flame is low enough).

Remove pan from the heat and put a couple of folded
towels under one side of it to tilt it toward you.

Pour the coconut shreds into a shallow dish.

Take an almond by the thin end, and carefully dip the
thick end into the hot honey, about a third of the way in.

Dip the honeyed end of the almond into the coconut
shreds, and put onto an ungreased baking sheet to cool.

Repeat with all the almonds. If the honey hardens, reheat
it momentarily.

Note:

You can use any leftover honey and coconut to make
a few *Coconut Balls* (see below).

COCONUT BALLS

Here's a quick and easy candy that's quite flexible.

honey   *desiccated coconut shreds*

In a small saucepan, simmer ½ cup honey or less for about 8 minutes (less time for less honey). Drip the honey over a cup or so of coconut shreds in a small bowl with sides.

Toss the mixture with a spoon, so that as much coconut as possible gets coated with honey.

Keep tossing until mixture is cool enough to handle. Then shape into balls or bars by rolling and pressing the mixture between the palms of your hands.

Note:
Return any unstuck coconut to the jar, or use for another recipe.

Brittles

Until we tried, we didn't know that you could make a peanut brittle at home, with honey instead of sugar. You can, and it's dynamite. But, honey makes up into a bit harder substance than granulated sugar and corn syrup do, so be forewarned when you bite into our *Peanut Brittle*.

A 7½-inch pan yields a brittle about ⅜ inch thick. For a thinner brittle, use an 8-inch pan, and add an additional ¼ cup peanuts.

PEANUT BRITTLE

We make this recipe with peanuts, but you can use any nuts, so long as you don't leave them in chunks larger than peanut size.

1 cup honey

1 cup shelled peanuts (skins on)

In a medium saucepan, cook the honey over a very low heat until it tests at "hard ball." (See beginning of this chapter for "Candy Testing.")

Lightly grease two baking pans, 7½ by 3½ inches (see "Greasing without Grease" chapter). Spread the shelled nuts over the bottoms of the two pans.

As soon as the honey tests "hard ball" pour it over the two pans—do not wait for the foam to settle, bubbles help to make candy lighter. You'll have to move the pot as you pour or the honey won't flow into all the corners. Scrape out the honey that sticks to the sides into the pans.

Allow the candy to cool very well, then turn it out of the pans as follows: put a large piece of waxed paper on a strong and solid flat surface—such as a stove top, or your floor. Pick up the pan, turn it over, and holding by the bottom, rap the topside of the pan down on the stovetop or floor, very flat and very sharply. You'll probably need a few raps to get it out.

Yield: about 50 square inches of brittle

MAPLE-WALNUT CHEWLE*

Maple syrup won't give you that very hard kind of candy that honey will, but it has properties all its own that are quite spectacular. For anyone who likes maple syrup, this is a must to try.

*1 cup maple syrup   1½ cups coarsely-chopped
                                              walnut nutmeats*

In a small saucepan, simmer the maple syrup for about 30 minutes, stirring occasionally, until it tests "medium-hard ball" (see beginning of this chapter for "Candy Testing").

Lightly grease two 8-inch loaf pans (see "Greasing without Grease" chapter) and spread the walnut chunks on the pan bottoms.

When cooked, immediately pour the syrup over the nuts, moving the pot as you pour, to get the ends and corners.

Allow to cool completely, then turn out as described in *Peanut Brittle* (above).   Yield: about 12 ounces

---

*Chewle—pronounced like brittle, but softer

Note:

At current prices, this delicious and mineral-rich candy costs us about $1.70 for the two panfuls.

MOLASSES-CASHEW CHEWLE

Barbados molasses is nowhere near as good a food as blackstrap. If you are a blackstrap fan, do substitute some blackstrap for the milder Barbados. But, if you've never tried blackstrap, begin by substituting a teaspoon at a time, or just stick to the basic recipe.

Cashew nuts have a sweetness which is just perfect with the molasses.

¾ cup Barbados molasses   1 cup raw cashews
¼ cup honey

Put the molasses and honey into a medium saucepan and simmer until the mixture tests at a "medium-hard ball" stage (see beginning of this chapter for "Candy Testing").

Meanwhile, lightly grease two 8-inch loaf pans (see "Greasing without Grease" chapter).

Break the cashews into halves lengthwise and spread out along the bottoms of the pans.

When cooked, pour the molasses-honey mixture over the nuts, moving the pot to get the syrup into the corners. (Do not wait for the bubbles to settle.)

Allow to cool very well, and then turn out as described in *Peanut Brittle* (above).

Yield: more than 60 square inches of *Chewle*

PRALINES

Here's another candy you pour, rather than handle hot.

Homemade *Pralines* are knockouts—the most delicious candy we know, and much easier to make than you'd think.

1 cup maple syrup   *½ cup pecan chunks*
½ cup supermilk*

In a medium saucepan, over a low heat, simmer the maple syrup about ½ hour until it reaches "soft ball" (see the beginning of this chapter for "Candy Testing").

Meanwhile, very lightly grease a large baking sheet (see "Greasing without Grease" chapter).

Divide the pecans into 8 portions and space out over the sheet in 8 low mounds.

When the syrup tests at "soft ball," add the milk, stir in well, and continue cooking until you reach the "medium-ball" stage.

Spoon the syrup-milk mixture over the piles of pecans, 1 tablespoon at a time, then divide up any remainder.

Allow to dry just on the top, then turn over with a spatula and allow to dry well on the other side—perhaps as long as overnight.

Yield: 8 large, delicious, glorious *Pralines*

FONDANT CARAMELS

Here is a recipe that is all in the handling.
You cannot do everything with it that you would do with sugar fondant, but it makes delicious caramels—and many of them. Don't hesitate to decrease the recipe if you have a small family.

2 cups honey

In a 3- or 4-quart pot bring the honey to a simmer, and cook about 30 minutes until it tests well into the "soft ball" stage (see beginning of this chapter for "Candy Testing"). Be sure you stir during the later stages of cooking.

---

*To make supermilk, mix together ⅓ cup water and ⅙ cup non-instant milk powder, or ⅓ cup whole milk and 1 heaping table-spoon noninstant milk powder, or ⅓ cup water and ⅓ cup instant milk powder.

Remove from the heat and, with a fork, beat in the pot for a few minutes, or until it looks creamy.

When cool enough to handle, spoon out half-teaspoonfuls and gently form into balls by hand. Put the balls onto a very-lightly greased dinner plate (see "Greasing without Grease" chapter).

As the balls cool and set, wrap each one gently in a piece of waxed paper, to keep them from spreading too far.

Yield: dozens

HONEY CREAMS

These are rather like *Caramels*, but richer.

1 cup honey	¼ cup noninstant milk
1 cup water	powder
	1 teaspoon vanilla extract

In a large saucepan, bring the honey to a simmer and allow it to cook over a very low heat until it tests at "soft ball" (see beginning of this chapter for "Candy Testing").

Meanwhile, very lightly grease a few dinner plates (see "Greasing without Grease" chapter).

Mix up the water, milk powder, and vanilla in a blender or shaker.

When the honey tests "soft ball," add the milk mixture to the honey and stir vigorously with a fork for about a minute. The milk will curdle, but that doesn't matter.

Bring to a simmer again and cook until the mixture tests again at "soft ball."

Remove from the heat and again stir vigorously with a fork for one minute. Allow to cool for a few minutes.

Spoon out teaspoonfuls onto the greased plates. Allow to cool until just warm. Roll between your hands, and wrap each piece in waxed paper.

Yield: about 30 candies

MAPLE CREAMS

Though these are made very much like the *Honey Creams*, they come out much more like "bon-bons."

1 cup maple syrup	*1 teaspoon vanilla or*
½ cup supermilk (see	*almond extract*
note on page 54)	*(optional)*
1½ teaspoons unsaturated	*pecan halves (optional)*
vegetable oil	

In a large saucepan, bring the maple syrup to a simmer and allow it to cook until it tests at "soft ball" (see the beginning of this chapter for "Candy Testing").

When at "soft ball" add the milk, oil and extract to the syrup.

Stir very well and frequently—don't worry about curdling. Cook until the mixture again tests at "soft ball."

Then, remove from the heat and stir very well.

When cool enough to handle, spoon out half-teaspoonfuls of the mixture and press onto a lightly-greased plate (see chapter on "Greasing without Grease"). If desired, press a pecan half into the top of each cream.

Yield: more than 24 creams

ANISE-HONEY CHEWS

If you think you've tasted it all, hang in there for a while. Here's a candy that's really terrific.

Star anise is easily ground in a blender, both seeds and pods together.

1 cup honey	*1½ teaspoons finely-ground*
	star anise

In a small saucepan, cook the honey and anise together over a low heat until the mixture tests at "medium ball" (see the beginning of this chapter for "Candy Testing").

Pour the mixture into a very-lightly greased soup bowl

(see chapter on "Greasing without Grease"). Allow to cool somewhat in the bowl.

When cool enough to handle, tear off bits and shape them into balls between the palms of your hands, then place them on a dry plate to set a bit more. When well set, wrap each piece in waxed paper.

Yield: about 24 chews

Note:
You can use any flavoring, herb, or spice in this manner.

MAPLE CHEWS

What can you say about maple syrup candies? For those of us who love the flavor of springtime and of maple syrup fresh from this year's boiling—everything else is second best.

We don't offer any alternatives to this candy—no variations or additions. Just maple syrup.

½ cup maple syrup

In a small saucepan, simmer the syrup over very low heat for about 10 minutes, until the syrup tests "medium ball" (see the beginning of this chapter for "Candy Testing").

Scrape out immediately into a lightly greased soup bowl (see chapter on "Greasing without Grease"). When the syrup has cooled down enough to handle, spoon out small amounts of it and roll them into balls between the palms of your hands.

Wrap each cooled ball in waxed paper.

Yield: about 12 chews

BUTTERSCOTCH CHEWS

We use real sweet butter in these recipes—not salted, not colored, and not margarine.

Adding butter to these chews gives them the really fine flavor and texture usually associated only with butterscotch.

Since we use butter as an ingredient, we *butter* the soup bowl we use for cooling.

½ *cup honey*   2   *tablespoons butter*

Put honey and butter into a small pot and simmer for about 12 minutes until the mixture tests at "medium ball" (see the beginning of this chapter for "Candy Testing").

Pour into a very-lightly-buttered soup bowl and allow to cool until it can be handled.

Spoon out teaspoonfuls of the candy and shape them between the palms of your hands. Sit them on a dry plate to cool further and set.

Wrap each piece in waxed paper for storage.

Yield: about 16 chews

CLOVE BUTTERSCOTCH CHEWS

A bit of ground clove gives the same recipe a delightful snap.

1   *recipe* Butterscotch   ½ *teaspoon ground*
     Chews *(see above)*   *cloves*

Make up as *Butterscotch Chews*.

Yield: about 16 chews

Fruit and Honey Candies

This group of candies is made like a very thick jam that hardens up to a chewy consistency.

Because you have to cook them down so much, they may come out quite dark, but don't let that put you off— keep the fire low and be patient. You'll still have some of the good orange and pineapple color when you finish. The pear, however, will probably darken no matter how slowly you cook it.

ORANGE CANDY

Use a California orange for this recipe. California oranges are usually not dyed.

This is a candy with real orange snap. If the zing is too much for you, next time cut the amount of orange peel in half—keeping all of the fruit, of course.

1 large navel orange   *½ cup honey*

Wash the orange well, trim, and cut into eight parts, peel and all. Liquefy in a blender.

Add the honey and blend again at medium speed.

Put the mixture into a medium saucepan and cook over very low heat, stirring occasionally until mixture is thick (cooking time will depend on the juiciness of the orange).

When thick, begin to stir constantly and vigorously until the mixture tests at "soft ball" (see the beginning of this chapter for "Candy Testing"), or until it begins to look like a thick sweet-potato mush.

Spoon half-teaspoonfuls onto a lightly-greased dish (see chapter on "Greasing without Grease").

When cool and set, wrap each piece in waxed paper.

Yield: about 24 small candies

PINEAPPLE CANDY

This candy takes about 1 hour to cook up—a long time, compared to many of the recipes we use—but it is worth every minute of it.

Grate the pineapple on the large-holed side of your old-fashioned grater; you want some bulk here, not just liquid pineapple.

1 cup peeled pineapple,   *¾ cup honey*
   grated

In a medium saucepan, cook the fruit and honey together over very low heat, until the mixture tests "soft ball" (see the beginning of this chapter for "Candy Testing").

Stir occasionally at the beginning, but constantly for the last few minutes of cooking. This stirring hastens the cooking. Cook it until all the free liquid is gone and the mixture looks quite thick.

Lightly grease a large dinner plate (see "Greasing without Grease" chapter), and spoon out half-tablespoonfuls of the candy. When candy has cooled slightly, smooth down any rough edges.

Wrap each piece in waxed paper, when candy is completely cooled.

Yield: about 24 magnificent candies

PEAR CANDY

Again, a long time—perhaps 75 minutes. But pear recipes seem to take longer.

These candies turn out the chewiest of the group.

¾ pound fresh pears   *¾ cup honey*

Wash and core, but do not peel, the pears. Cube them small, skin and all.

Put pears into a pot with the honey and simmer about 1 hour and 15 minutes, until mixture tests at "soft ball" (see the beginning of this chapter for "Candy Testing").

Lightly grease a large dinner plate (see "Greasing without Grease" chapter) and spoon out small amounts of candy onto the plate.

When somewhat cooled, smooth with your fingers.

When completely cooled, wrap each piece in waxed paper.

Yield: about 24 candies

Honey Suckers

These are a logical step after chewy honey candies. You just cook the honey one step further to the "hard-ball" stage. (See the beginning of this chapter for "Candy Testing.")

Once they are cooked, though, rather than just spoon

out candy-sized bits, we treat them somewhat like taffy—until they harden.

The pulling and cutting we go through gives the finished sucker an airy texture and a lighter color that are pleasing.

When the ingredients have reached the "hard-ball" stage, pour the hot candy into a lightly-greased soup bowl (see "Greasing without Grease" chapter). Allow candy to cool down until it can be picked up in the hand without burning you (it should come out of the bowl quite readily). This requires a bit of judgment because if you pick it up too hot it burns, and if you wait until the candy's too cool it won't pull into strands.

Pick up the warm candy, and pull it into a thick strand. Fold the ends in over one another, and pull again. Keep repeating this until you can feel the honey hardening.

Before it really hardens, pull and roll the candy into a long strand about as thick as your pinky finger. Take a sharp knife and cut the strand into about 1-inch pieces.

When cut, wrap each piece in waxed paper. They will keep almost indefinitely.

We only give you a few variations, but all the chews given earlier except *Maple Chews* will, if cooked further, go on to become suckers.

LEMON-HONEY SUCKERS

½ cup honey   ¼ cup fresh lemon juice

Cook as described in *Honey Suckers* (see above).

Yield: about 16 suckers

CINNAMON-HONEY SUCKERS

½ cup honey   1 teaspoon powdered
                                 cinnamon

Cook as described in *Honey Suckers* (see above).

Yield: about 16 suckers

HONEY-MOLASSES SUCKERS

You need no flavoring beyond the flavor of the black-strap. The combination is really delicious, even if you don't like the taste of blackstrap.

¼ *cup blackstrap molasses*   ¼ *cup honey*

Cook as described in *Honey Suckers* (see above).

Yield: about 16 suckers

Turkish Delight

One complication with *Turkish Delight* is the waxed-paper tray you must fold and clip together to hold it in after cooking and before powdering. This tray gets cut up and discarded in the finishing of the candy.

CINNAMON TURKISH DELIGHT

The Turks had cinnamon, but most *Turkish Delight* is fruit-flavored rather than spiced. That makes this recipe doubly unusual.

You'll come across arrowroot starch in our "Puddings" chapter. It is flavorless, and disappears in the cooking. But here we also use the arrowroot starch to powder the outsides of our still-sticky candy. The arrowroot looks just like confectioners' sugar.

Have a large scissors handy, clean enough to cut through the gelled candy after it is well cooled.

¼ *cup hot water*   ¼ *teaspoon ground*
½ *cup honey*   *cinnamon*
                           2 *rounded tablespoons*
                                arrowroot starch

Combine all the ingredients in a 1-quart saucepan and mix well with a fork, to dissolve the arrowroot. Prepare a waxed-paper tray as described below and dust its bottom and sides with a bit more arrowroot. (Don't put away the bottle of arrowroot starch—you'll need more.)

Cook the honey mixture over medium heat, stirring constantly, until it gets very thick, about 3 to 5 minutes. The mixture should be too thick to pour—you should have to spoon it out. If the mixture refuses to thicken, you probably haven't used enough arrowroot. Mix an additional tablespoon with ¼ cup of warm water (in the blender or mixer), add it to the cooked mixture, and stir it in—then cook some more, until thick.

To make the waxed paper tray:

Take a piece of waxed paper about 18″ long, and fold it in half (to make it 9″ long);

Fold the sides in to meet in the middle;

Turn the paper over so the folds face down;

Fold up about 1″ of all 4 edges;

Bend up the edges, allowing the corners to be *outside;*

With paper clips, clip the corners to the sides;

Dust the inside of the completed tray with a bit of the starch.

When cooked, spoon the mixture out of the saucepan and into the powdered, waxed-paper tray. Allow it to cool for about 1 hour. The mixture will not *fill* the tray. Don't try to even out the top. The candy is still very sticky.

When cool, dust the top of the candy with a little more arrowroot starch.

When the top is dusted, remove the paper clips from the corners of the tray.

Take your clean large scissors and *cut* the set mixture into 1-inch strips, lengthwise, setting the strips on a clean surface. Pick up one of the strips by an end of waxed paper, and peel the paper away from the candy—this new surface will be wet, so lay the candy, powdered side down, on a clean plate. (Once you have the stuff in front of you, all this becomes very clear.)

When you've peeled the paper away from all the strips, lightly dust the damp parts with more arrowroot.

Pick up each strip and cut it into 1-inch pieces, laying the pieces back on the plate. Pour a little more starch into your hand and dust the new edges. Make certain all the surfaces of the candy have a *light* dusting of starch on them.

Yield: about 12 delightful candies

LEMON TURKISH DELIGHT

This candy has real lemon flavor.

¼ cup fresh lemon juice	¼ cup hot water
¾ cup honey	3 rounded tablespoons arrowroot starch

In a 1-quart saucepan, mix all the ingredients together very well, and prepare as in *Cinnamon Turkish Delight* (see above).

Yield: 12 candies

ORANGE-NUT TURKISH DELIGHT

Turkish Delight is even more elegant with nuts in it. Feel free to add nuts to either of the other *Turkish Delight* recipes, too.

⅓ cup fresh orange juice	2½ rounded tablespoons arrowroot starch
¾ cup honey	¼ cup filberts, in halves and quarters
⅛ cup hot water	

In a 1-quart saucepan, mix all the ingredients together very well, and prepare as described in *Cinnamon Turkish Delight* (see above).

Yield: 12 candies

5

Crackers

Most of the crackers on the market are made with white flour—bleached and brominated. Some crackers are made with both whole wheat and white flour. A few are made of whole wheat or whole rye or other grains which are wholesome and not highly processed. But you still have the questions of freshness, use of preservatives, cleanliness and truthfulness.

We make our own crackers. Sometimes out of wheat and sometimes not. Those of you who are allergic to wheat (and rye), will find here crackers made solely of rice. Those of you who can't have any grains at all, will find crackers made of potatoes.

We find it rewarding to make our own crackers—they keep well, wrapped in plastic bags, and they have marvelous textures. However, since we never use white flour we are unable to make a cracker as light as the very light commercial kinds.

RICE CRISPS

This isn't so much a recipe as it is a principle.

You can find these under various names in the gourmet and specialty groceries, but we make them here without a lot of salt, without oil, without MSG—and we make them fresh.

You'll need waxed paper and a rolling pin for these.

Now, the technique for rolling *Rice Crisps* thin isn't quite as complicated as playing the violin, but you perfect it the same way that a violinist gets to Carnegie Hall: "practice." These crackers are worth the effort.

Cooking Short-Grain Brown Rice

Use 1 cup of short-grain brown rice (we like the flavor, the texture, and the lower price of the short grain) to 3 cups of hot water and a teaspoon or so of salt, to taste. Bring the water and salt to a vigorous boil, add the rice, and reduce the heat to simmering. Stir once, cover the pot, and cook for about 45 minutes or until quite tender. For eating you might want the rice a bit more *al dente,* but for these recipes you want it rather soft. One cup of raw rice should yield about 2½ cups of cooked rice.

BASIC RICE CRISPS

Here's the place to master the technique.

1 cup cooked short-grain   *salt (optional)*
brown rice (see "Cooking
Short-Grain Brown Rice,"
above)

Measure the rice into a bowl and mash for a moment or so with a fork or potato masher. Taste for salt.

Lightly grease a large baking sheet (see "Greasing without Grease" chapter).

Tear off a sheet of waxed paper the length of the baking sheet and place it on a flat surface (we use the top of our enamelled kitchen table).

Spoon the rice mush into the middle of the paper and flatten it with your hand. Cover it with another sheet of waxed paper about the same size and, with a rolling pin, roll rice into a large rectangle. Roll as thin as you can, without going through the rice.

When rolled out, gently peel off the top waxed paper. The rice may stick a little bit, but not much.

Carrying it by the bottom piece of paper, bring the rolled-out rice to the greased baking sheet, and quickly turn the paper over onto the pan.

Gently peel off the wax paper. If the rice sticks in spots, as it is prone to do, help it off with a knife as you pull off the paper. You want to finish with one large sheet of rice.

Once it is off the paper and onto the pan, score the rice with a sharp knife into rectangular cracker shapes.

Bake at low temperature (about 300°) until brown and crisp, about 45 minutes.

Yield: about twenty-five 2- by 2-inch crackers

ONION CRISPS

Actually, once you begin to add dry ingredients, such as the onion flakes, the rice becomes less sticky and easier to handle.

1 cup cooked short-grain brown rice (see "Cooking Short-Grain Brown Rice," above)

½ teaspoon dried onion flakes

Mash the onion flakes in well with the cooked rice.

Prepare and bake as in *Basic Rice Crisps* (see above).

Yield: about 25

KELP CRISPS

Granulated (or powdered) kelp is a dynamite source of iodine. This is especially important for those of us who use sea salt instead of supermarket iodized salt. Sea salt has no iodine in it, and so a supplement is necessary.

However, if you're not used to the taste of kelp (that is, if you've never kelped before), reduce the amount called for to 1 teaspoon.

This Crisp tastes delicious with cottage cheese.

1 cup cooked short-grain   2 teaspoons granulated kelp
brown rice (see "Cooking
Short-Grain Brown Rice,"
above)

Mix the kelp in with the mashed rice.

Prepare and bake as in *Basic Rice Crisps* (see above).

Yield: about 25

SESAME CRISPS

The sesame seeds should be unhulled. They look whiter than the hulled seeds, but they keep their oils fresher longer that way. This is an excellent flavor, reminiscent of some of the better commercial crackers.

3 tablespoons unhulled   1 cup cooked short-grain
sesame seeds   brown rice (see "Cooking
                                   Short-Grain Brown Rice,"
                                   above)

Mix and bake as in *Basic Rice Crisps* (see above).

Yield: about 25

SWEET CRISPS

This makes a delightful sweet cracker. Keep your nose on the watch (so to speak) with this cracker. Coconut seems to have a tendency to scorch.

¼ cup desiccated coconut   1 cup cooked short-grain
shreds   brown rice (see "Cook-
                                   ing Short-Grain Brown
                                   Rice," above)

Mix together very well.

Prepare and bake as in *Basic Rice Crisps* (see above).

Yield: about 25

LIVER AND ONION CRISPS

No, it's not a joke. This recipe really works, using fresh

liver, and comes out tasting not at all like liver—we asked our resident liver-hater.

1 cup cooked short-grain brown rice (see "Cooking Short-Grain Brown Rice," above)	1 ounce fresh liver (peel off the skin before weighing)
	2 teaspoons dried onion flakes

Measure the cooked rice into a medium mixing bowl.

Grind the bit of liver well in your blender, or chop it well with a crescent chopper.

Add the liver and the onion flakes to the rice and mix very well.

Prepare and bake as in *Basic Rice Crisps* (see above).

Yield: about 25

SALT-FREE CRISPS

Just prepare as you would *Basic Rice Crisps* (see above), but leave the salt out of the cooking rice. You can use a potassium chloride salt-substitute, but if you're used to little or no salt, the rice can have a very nutlike flavor.

Yield: about 25

RICE-BRAN CRISPS

Rice bran is the outer hulls of brown rice—the part that gets ground off in turning brown into white rice. It can be bought at Oriental food stores as well as in health food stores, and it is a very good source of B vitamins.

Rice bran also helps to make this one of the easiest Crisps recipes to prepare: it makes the mush much drier (say that very fast 10 times).

These come out especially crisp and flaky, but be warned that some folks find rice bran a little bitter.

1 cup cooked short-grain brown rice (see "Cooking Short-Grain Brown Rice," above)	2 tablespoons fine rice bran

Prepare and bake as in *Basic Rice Crisps* (see above).
Yield: about 25

GREEN CRISPS

Greens are good for you (so eat your collards and stop crying).

1 stalk collard greens (or 2 spinach leaves)	1 cup cooked short-grain brown rice (see "Cook-
½ teaspoon caraway seeds	ing Short-Grain Brown Rice," above)

Grind the greens with your grater as fine as you can get them.

Add them with the seeds to the rice, and prepare and bake as in *Basic Rice Crisps* (see above).

Yield: about 25

CHEESE CRISPS

You always have to be particularly careful with cheese crackers—they have a tendency to scorch and stick. So use a bit more grease (see "Greasing without Grease" chapter) than you would for the other recipes.

1 cup cooked short-grain brown rice (see "Cook- ing Short-Grain Brown Rice," above)	1 ounce grated uncolored sharp cheese
	½ teaspoon dried onion flakes

Measure your rice into a bowl.

With a fork, mash the cheese and onions into rice until mixture is uniform.

Prepare and bake as in *Basic Rice Crisps* (see above).

Yield: about 25

Note:
These are only a few of the myriads of possible variations.

POTATO CRISPS

These crisps don't have any fat in them, so they are much more potato-tasting than potato chips are. So, if you like the potatoes, but not the heavy fat and the excess salt, in potato chips, this is a cracker for you.

Since cooked potatoes are not as solid as cooked rice, they are more difficult to handle. And, if they scorch, or even really brown in these recipes, they tend to get bitter. The browner, the bitterer. So, in baking them, check frequently to make certain they're not getting scorched. If your oven gives uneven heat (as ours does), you may want to remove the more done ones from the batch and let the paler ones cook on—it's silly to be stubborn and insist that the whole batch must come out at the same time, and wind up with some done and some bitter.

1 packed cup cooked
   potatoes, with skins
	½ teaspoon caraway seeds
	   salt, to taste

In a mixing bowl, mash the potatoes with a masher or fork and mix the seeds in well. Taste for salt.

Work potatoes for a minute with your hands until the potatoes are smooth, then place on an enamelled (or Formica) tabletop, or on a marble kneading board. Flatten slightly with your hand.

Cover with a large sheet of waxed paper, and roll out quite thin and even.

Peel off the paper, but don't discard it: you'll want to use it again.

Grease a large baking sheet (see "Greasing without Grease" chapter).

Now, take a round cookie cutter or a drinking glass about 3 inches across and cut out rounds of the flattened potatoes, the same way you would cut out cookies.

Remove the excess.

With a pancake turner, lift each round off the table, and place it on the baking sheet. If the rounds stick to the turner, give a flip and turn the turner over, dropping the round not on the floor, but on the sheet.

When all the rounds are on the sheet, knead up the excess briefly, cover again with the waxed paper, and roll out.

Repeat the process until all the rounds are on the baking sheet.

Bake at medium (about 350°) for about 25 to 30 minutes.

Try one of the crackers before you remove them from the oven. They won't come out as crisp as *Rice Crisps,* but, remember, you don't want to really brown these or they may go bitter on you.   Yield: about 17

ONION-POTATO CRISPS

2 tablespoons dried onion   1 packed cup cooked
  flakes   potatoes, with skins
1 teaspoon poppy seeds

Mix, mash, roll, and bake as *Potato Crisps* (see above).
Yield: about 18

Grain Crackers

Here they are: wheat, rye, corn, and oats.

SIMPLE WHOLE WHEAT CRACKERS

These are not risen crackers. So they must be thin. If they are not thin, you can use them as shingles or siding, but not to eat. In order to roll them thin, you must *knead in only enough flour to be able to handle the dough and roll it out.*

We have found that a large cookie sheet without sides is the best pan for these crackers. They get their final rolling right on the sheet.

½ cup water   ⅞ cup whole wheat flour
½ teaspoon salt   (approximately)

In a mixing bowl, mix together the water, salt, and enough flour to make a moist dough, but one which will roll out without sticking. Knead for only a few minutes until dough is quite cohesive.

Roll out on a floured board. Turn the dough over several times during the rolling, and flour your board as needed. These steps will help insure that your dough doesn't stick.

Finally, put the half-rolled dough on the cookie sheet, and *roll it very thin.* (Now you don't care about sticking.)

Score with a sharp knife into 2-inch rectangular shapes, and bake in a medium oven (about 350°) until crisp, about 30 minutes.

Yield: about 25

WHOLE WHEAT SESAME CRACKERS

Not only are sesame seeds tasty and nutritious, but they also help dough roll out more easily—prevent the dough from sticking as much.

¾ cup water	1½ cups whole wheat flour
¼ teaspoon salt	½ cup unhulled sesame seeds

Make up the dough and knead in the sesame seeds.

Knead a few minutes only, until quite cohesive.

Roll out dough somewhat, flouring as you need to, and turning the dough frequently to keep it from sticking.

Grease a large cookie sheet (see "Greasing without Grease" chapter), transfer the half-rolled dough to the sheet, and roll out very thin (no need to turn now).

Score with a sharp knife into rectangles and bake in a medium oven (about 350°) about 30 minutes or until crisp.

Yield: about 36

CHEESE FLATS

Cheese crackers are always exciting, but don't expect them to come out that orange-yellow color of the commercial cracker. They use dyed cheeses. There are many wholesome undyed cheeses on the market.

These are crackers only by our definition: they could just as easily be called snacks. But they *can* be used as a something on which to put something else—hence, we call them crackers.

Because you broil rather than bake these, they require less cooking time.

3 ounces uncolored sharp cheddar cheese	1 egg white (see "Separating Eggs" in the "Cakes" chapter)
1 whole large egg	¼ cup whole wheat flour salt and pepper, to taste

Grate the cheese into a mixing bowl, add the remaining ingredients, mix very well, and taste for additional salt or pepper.

Spoon half teaspoonfuls onto a greased baking sheet (see "Greasing without Grease" chapter), leaving room between for a good deal of spreading.

Broil at medium high heat for about 12 minutes, until light brown and quite spread.

Turn and broil on the other side for about 2 *minutes* (don't scorch).

Yield: about 20 flats

CORN DODGER (or Corn Pone)

Corn is a delicious grain, but difficult to shape into crackers. Corn kernels, intact, last for years, still holding their ability to sprout into live plants. However, once you break the protective outer coating and grind it, the corn quickly loses its flavor.

We grind our own corn in our blender, and that works

just fine, giving us fresh-ground cornmeal, 1 cup at a time, when we want to use it. We never grind in advance: that would not be as bad as buying ground cornmeal, but not as good as grinding as needed. If you do grind extra cornmeal, refrigerate it.

If you must buy ground cornmeal, at least buy cornmeal that is whole, not degerminated.

These are thick for crackers, and chewy, but really more flavorful than wheat crackers.

1¼	cups fresh-ground cornmeal (or 1⅛ cups corn berries, for grinding)	½	teaspoon salt
		1	teaspoon unsaturated vegetable oil
		¾	cup boiling water

In a mixing bowl, mix the cornmeal and salt together.

Bring the oil and water to a boil in a small saucepan, and then pour over the meal. Stir *very* well.

Grease a large baking sheet (see "Greasing without Grease" chapter).

Pick up handfuls of meal and shape into ¼-inch-thick cakes. Place the cakes on the baking sheet. They can almost touch, as there will be no rise or spreading.

Starting in a cold oven, bake at 375° to 400° for 25 to 30 minutes, or until the bottoms are brown.

Yield: 1 panful

CORN CRACKERS

The cracker you get from this recipe largely depends on how thin you can roll out the cornmeal.

Remember, cornmeal batter doesn't have the cohesion of a wheat dough, so handle it much more gently.

1	cup fresh-ground cornmeal	¾	teaspoon salt
		½	cup boiling water

In a mixing bowl, mix together the cornmeal and salt.

Pour the boiling water over the meal and stir well.

Grease a large baking sheet (see "Greasing without Grease" chapter).

Shape the mixture into a rough ball and place on the baking sheet. With a rolling pin, roll the mixture as thin as you can, without going right through it.

Score into small rectangles with a sharp knife.

Bake in medium oven (about 350°) until crisp and brown (but watch out for scorching, especially if you've almost gone through in spots). Baking time depends on the thickness of your cornmeal mixture, but start checking after 20 minutes.
Yield: about 25

Variation:
    Vary this cracker with almost any seed, or with the variations we gave with *Rice Crisps* (see page 67–70).

CARAWAY YEAST CRACKERS

You don't get a lot of rise from the yeast in this cracker—just enough to make it slightly softer than unrisen crackers.

You'll have to plan ahead for this recipe: it requires at least a few hours of rising.

Any of your favorite yeast-bread recipes can be adapted to crackers, if you follow these instructions.

1	tablespoon active dry yeast	1½ to 1⅞	cups whole wheat flour
½	cup hot tap water	1	teaspoon caraway seeds
½	teaspoon salt		

Mix all the ingredients together in a medium-sized mixing bowl and knead up the dough for a few minutes until it is moist and cohesive.

Scrape the bowl down and shape the dough into a ball. Return the ball to the bowl, cover the bowl with a damp towel, and set it in a warm location for a couple of hours for the dough to rise quite high.

When risen, knead down and roll out half thin.

Grease a large cookie sheet (see "Greasing without Grease" chapter) and place the dough on it. Roll out until it is quite thin, then score with a knife into rectangles.

Cover with a clean *dry* towel and put back in that warm place for about ½ hour.

Starting in a cold oven, set the heat at very low (this allows some last-minute rising to take place) and bake for about 15 minutes. Increase the heat to medium (about 350°) and bake for another 20 to 30 minutes, until brown and crisp.

Yield: about 40 crackers

OATMEAL CRACKERS

Oatmeal is not as protein-rich a grain as wheat, but it has a distinctive texture that many love.

1 tablespoon active dry yeast	1 teaspoon dried onion flakes
½ teaspoon salt	1½ cups rolled oats
½ cup hot tap water	

In a mixing bowl, mix the yeast with the salt and hot water, and stir a bit.

Add the onion flakes and as much of the oatmeal as is needed to make a "dough."

Grease a large baking sheet (see "Greasing without Grease" chapter).

Put the oatmeal mixture on the baking sheet, and with a rolling pin roll it out to about ⅛ inch or less.

Cover with a clean dry towel and set in a warm place for about 1 hour to rise a bit. Don't look for rise. It's too slight to be visible. But it doesn't take much rise to lighten the cracker, which is what we're looking for.

After the hour, remove towel and place baking sheet in a cold oven. Set heat for very low (under 250°) and bake for 15 minutes. Raise the heat to medium (about 350°)

and bake until crisp and done—perhaps another 15 minutes.

Yield: about 30

RYE CRACKERS

Rye has a great flavor, very distinctive and a little sour. It is more difficult to use for breads than wheat flour because it stays sticky for so long—then by the time you've kneaded enough flour in to stop the sticking, you've got heavy bread. But with crackers, we don't have to worry about the stickiness or the long-distance kneading.

By the way, without special ovens and rolling machines, you can't get rye crackers as light as some of the commercial crackers you can buy, but the commercial ones can't touch these for flavor.

1	tablespoon active dry yeast	1	teaspoon caraway seeds
½	teaspoon salt	1⅛	cups stone-ground whole rye flour
½	cup hot tap water		

In a mixing bowl, mix together the yeast, salt, and hot water; add the seeds and flour, and mix until you have a cohesive ball.

Roll, rise, and bake, as in the recipe for *Oatmeal Crackers*.

Yield: about 30

Note:

Remember, texture and baking time really depends on you being able to roll your crackers thin.

Soda Crackers

In these recipes (as in other recipes we do with baking soda), we use a small amount of baking soda, which should be completely neutralized by the acidic yoghurt (or sour milk or buttermilk, if you prefer). By the time you eat it, there is no alkalizing power left in the soda.

The baking soda will, however, leave sodium residues

in the crackers, so, if you are on a sodium-restricted diet avoid them.

CHEESE SODA SQUARES

Please use only uncolored cheeses. The colored ones are dyed.

½ cup water	½ teaspoon salt
1 rounded tablespoon yoghurt	½ teaspoon baking soda
1½ cups whole wheat flour	2 ounces sharp un-colored cheese

Into a mixing bowl measure the water, yoghurt, flour, salt, and soda, and mix very well.

Grate the cheese over the mixture and stir in well.

Shape it all into a rough ball, remove ball from the bowl, and set on a floured surface to roll out. To avoid sticking while rolling, turn frequently and flour as needed. Roll out dough to about ¼-inch thick.

Grease a large cookie sheet (see "Greasing without Grease" chapter).

Place the dough on the sheet and roll out quite thin— about ⅛ inch.

Bake at medium temperature (about 350°) 25 to 30 minutes until crisp.
Yield: about 36
minutes until crisp.   Yield: about 36

Note: Try varying the recipe by adding 2 tablespoons of sesame seeds during the mixing.

SOFT SPINACH SODAS

Here's a different cracker—soft and chewy, rather than hard and crisp. Also, this cracker is not rolled smooth, but rather spooned out and smoothed only as smooth as a spoon can make it.

Your blender is an excellent tool for making green vegetables usable in a dough.

½	cup water	½	teaspoon baking soda
2	cups (not packed) fresh spinach	1	rounded tablespoon yoghurt
1	teaspoon fennel seed	1¼	cups whole wheat flour
½	teaspoon salt		

Into your blender measure the water, spinach, seeds, salt, and baking soda, and blend at medium speed until you have a puree.

Measure the yoghurt and flour into a mixing bowl, pour the blender mixture over it, and stir well, until uniform. Grease a baking sheet (see "Greasing without Grease" chapter).

Scrape batter onto the sheet and spread with the back of a spoon to a depth of about ¼ inch.

With a knife, score the batter into squares.

Bake at 400° to 450° for about 20 to 25 minutes, or until browning on top.
Yield: 25 to 30

A No-Grain Cracker

If you can't eat any grain at all, this cracker is for you. It is sweet, though, so *not* a cracker to serve with sharp cheese and onions.

SUNFLOWER-SEED CRACKERS

This is not a cracker *with* sunflower seeds, it is a cracker *of* sunflower seeds. It is a crazy idea that worked out beautifully.

| 1 | cup hulled sunflower seeds | ½ | cup desiccated coconut shreds |
| | | ¼ | cup cold water |

In a blender or mill, grind the seeds until you get a flour. In a mixing bowl, mix together all the ingredients for a few minutes until you have a cohesive ball.

Grease a large baking sheet (see "Greasing without Grease" chapter).

Place the ball on the sheet and flatten it with your hand.

Place a large piece of waxed paper over the flattened ball and roll it out with a rolling pin until it is quite thin.

Remove the paper and score the dough into rectangular shapes with sharp knife.

Starting in a cold oven, bake at medium-low temperature about ¾ hour until brown.   Yield: about 25

6

Muffins and Biscuits

For years Stan stayed away from biscuits and muffins because he didn't like the "chemical" taste. The chemical taste in most of these baked goods comes from baking powder, an ingredient eliminated from these recipes and from our cake recipes too. Yes, baking soda can taste "chemicalish" too, but the baking soda works on a different principle and its taste disappears in baking. If you find a chemical taste in your muffins or biscuits (or cakes), you are using either too much soda or too little yoghurt (see "Cakes" chapter).

What is the difference between biscuits and muffins? In our definition, muffins have sweetener and biscuits don't. Muffins have a light texture, and biscuits have a heavy, chewy texture. Made light enough, muffins come close to cupcakes.

But the differences don't really matter: both are treats, special dishes that don't belong at every meal. That's why our recipes yield so few. These treats are much more tempting than plain breads are. So, we make only as many as we want to eat, here and now. After all, a couple of muffins each is enough. They aren't supposed to be the whole meal.

Of course, if you have a large family, go ahead and double the recipes.

BRAN MUFFINS

Preheat oven: 350° (medium)

Here's a traditional introduction to muffins. The flavor is rich and the texture excellent.

We were on a camping trip on Prince Edward Island in Canada one spring, and inclement weather forced us into a guest house. We were served homemade bran muffins, which the lady of the house made from bran that the nearby mill was discarding as waste. Do *you* live near a mill?

1 cup whole wheat flour	1½ tablespoons molasses
½ cup fine wheat bran	¼ teaspoon salt
½ teaspoon baking soda	1 cup yoghurt

Grease a 6-cup muffin pan (see "Greasing without Grease" chapter).

Measure the flour, bran, and soda into a bowl. Mix with a fork until very well distributed.

Add the remaining ingredients and mix well.

Divide batter among the cups of your muffin tin (we mean the metal cups, not paper muffin liners).

Bake in preheated oven at medium to medium-high temperature (350° to 375°), for about 30 minutes, or until the muffins test done (see page 161, "Testing"). Yield: 6

WHOLE WHEAT MUFFINS

Preheat oven: 350° (medium)

We make *Whole Wheat Muffins* when we don't have any bran, but for our taste they don't have the fine flavor of *Bran Muffins*.

1½ cups whole wheat flour	¼ teaspoon salt
½ teaspoon baking soda	1 cup yoghurt
2 tablespoons honey	

Grease a 6-cup muffin pan (see "Greasing without Grease" chapter).

Measure the flour and soda into a medium-sized mixing bowl. Mix with a fork until well distributed. Add the honey, salt and yoghurt and mix well.

Divide batter among the cups of your muffin tin (we mean the metal cups, not paper muffin liners).

Bake in preheated oven for about 30 minutes, or until the muffins test done (see "Testing," page 147).

Yield: 6

CORN MUFFINS

Preheat oven: 350° (medium)

Fresh-ground cornmeal is important to really corn-tasting corn muffins. The packaged cornmeal bought from supermarket shelves just can't compare (see "Ingredients" chapter for more on cornmeal). We grind our own corn-meal in our blender. Put a cup of corn berries in the con-tainer of your blender (these kernels don't have to be fresh—in the hull they stay wholesome for a long time). Blend at high speed until the corn is all ground down into meal. A cup of corn gives you a little more than a cup of meal.

In this recipe, start out with 1⅜ cups of berries for 1½ cups of meal.

1 egg	¼ teaspoon salt
½ cup yoghurt	½ teaspoon baking
2 tablespoons unsaturated	soda
vegetable oil	1½ cups fresh-ground
2 tablespoons honey	cornmeal

In a mixing bowl, mix together the egg, yoghurt, oil, honey and salt.

Add the baking soda and mix very well.

Stir the cornmeal in well.

Allow the mixture to stand for 5 minutes (to soften any larger pieces of corn left in the meal).

Grease a 6-cup muffin tray (see "Greasing without

Grease" chapter) and divide the batter among the cups.

Bake in a preheated oven at medium temperature (about 350°) for 20 to 25 minutes. Test for doneness (see page 147, "Testing").

Yield: 6

100 PERCENT RYE MUFFINS

Preheat oven: 325° (medium-low)

We didn't believe you could get muffins this light from only rye flour. We knew rye flour was tasty, but it is also usually heavy.

If you've got problems with wheat and don't like corn, here's your chance.

¼ teaspoon salt	2 tablespoons unsaturated
½ teaspoon baking soda	vegetable oil
1 large egg	½ cup yoghurt
1 tablespoon honey	1 cup rye flour

In a mixing bowl, mix together the salt, baking soda, and egg.

Add the honey, oil and yoghurt. Stir very well.

Mix the flour in well.

Grease a 6-cup muffin pan (see "Greasing without Grease" chapter) and divide the batter among the cups.

Bake in a preheated oven at medium-low temperature (about 325°) for 25 to 30 minutes, or until the muffins test done (see page 147, "Testing").

Yield: 6

BLUEBERRY MUFFINS

Preheat oven: 350° (medium)

One of the pleasures we get out of cooking and writing cookbooks is preparing traditional dishes in an untraditional manner. Here's a good example.

The blueberries we prefer to use are wild blueberries,

but they are tart—hence the amount of honey. If you use sweeter berries, you might want to reduce the amount of honey by 1 tablespoon.

1 large egg	¼ teaspoon salt
¾ cup yoghurt	1 teaspoon baking soda
2 tablespoons unsaturated vegetable oil	1 cup wild blueberries
	1 cup whole wheat flour
¼ cup honey	

In a mixing bowl, mix together the egg, yoghurt, oil, honey, and salt. Stir well.

Stir in the baking soda until it is well distributed.

Mix in the berries.

Add the flour and mix until well distributed.

Grease an 8-cup muffin pan (see "Greasing without Grease" chapter). Divide the batter among the 8 cups.

Bake in preheated oven at medium temperature (about 350°) for about 30 minutes, or until the muffins test done (see page 147, "Testing").

Yield: 8 very large muffins

PINEAPPLE MUFFINS

Preheat oven: 350° (medium)

Don't ask us how to convert this recipe so you can use canned pineapple. We haven't bought a canned food in years. (We would have cooperated with the ecology drives, but we just didn't have any tin cans to contribute.) And years ago, when we did buy some canned foods, pineapple was not one of our biggies. The same acid that makes for great flavor in fresh pineapple seems to react against the metal of cans, making an unpleasant flavor.

If a fruit is not available fresh, substitute another. You could make this same recipe with apple, for example. As far as our cooking is concerned, if we can't get it fresh, canned is banned. We make something else.

The acid flavor of the pineapple is quite striking against the sweetness of the muffin.

Do cut the pineapple into small chunks: too-large chunks can make a muffin fall apart.

1	large egg	¼	teaspoon salt
½	cup yoghurt	½	teaspoon baking soda
2	tablespoons unsaturated vegetable oil	½	cup small-diced fresh pineapple
2	tablespoons honey	1¼	cups whole wheat flour

Break the egg into a large mixing bowl and whisk lightly.

Add the yoghurt, oil, honey, and salt. Stir well.

Blend in the baking soda.

Mix in the pineapple chunks.

Add the flour and stir the batter quite well.

Grease 10 cups of 2 muffin pans (see "Greasing without Grease" chapter) and spoon in the batter.

Bake in preheated oven at medium temperature (about 350°) for 25 to 30 minutes, or until the muffins test done (see page 147, "Testing").

Yield: 10

YEAST MUFFINS

If you don't want to use any baking soda at all, not even the minimal amounts we use, here's a recipe for you. These muffins require a good deal more time (not much more work but a lot more time), but they have an excellent texture and a fine flavor.

They need 18 hours of rising time. The handy thing about this recipe is that you have it all mixed the day before. So all you have to do is spoon and bake. If you want these in the morning before leaving the house, mix the dough the afternoon before.

1	large egg	¼	teaspoon salt
1	tablespoon active dry yeast	1½	tablespoons unsaturated vegetable oil
½	cup yoghurt	1	cup whole wheat flour
1	tablespoon honey		

In a large mixing bowl mix together the egg, yeast, yoghurt, honey, salt and oil, stirring very well.

Mix in the flour and beat with a spoon for a minute.

Cover with a damp towel (at least it should be damp to begin with). Set in a warm place to rise for 18 hours. After that length of time, beat the batter down with a spoon.

Grease a 6-cup muffin pan (see "Greasing without Grease" chapter) and spoon in the batter.

Start muffins in a cold oven and bake for about 40 minutes at about 300° (low). The cold start and low temperature give the yeast a chance to raise the muffins.

Yield: 6

CHEESE YEAST MUFFINS

A good recipe is worth a good variation. The cheese makes this muffin delightfully crisp.

1 recipe Yeast Muffins *(above)*	*¼ pound uncolored, sharp cheddar cheese*
	1 large egg (additional)

Follow the recipe for *Yeast Muffins* up to greasing the muffin pan.

When ready to bake, grate the cheese over the batter, break in the additional egg, and stir very well.

Grease a 6-cup muffin pan (see "Greasing without Grease" chapter) and spoon in the batter.

Start muffins in a cold oven and bake for about 40 minutes at 300° (low). The cold start and low temperature give the yeast a chance to rise.

Yield: 6

WHOLE WHEAT SODA BISCUITS

Preheat oven: 400° (high)

These don't have the cakelike texture of muffins, but they do have a pleasant roughness to them.

2 tablespoons unsaturated vegetable oil	½ teaspoon salt
	¾ teaspoon baking soda
¾ cup yoghurt	1¾ cups whole wheat flour

Mix together the oil, yoghurt, and salt in a mixing bowl.

Add the baking soda and mix very well.

Mix in the flour until the batter is uniform.

Shape into ¾-inch rounds and place on a greased baking sheet (see "Greasing without Grease" chapter).

Bake in preheated oven at 400° for about 25 minutes (or until done). The only way to really test a biscuit for doneness is to break one open.

Yield: 8 to 10

CHEESE WHEAT-GERM BISCUITS

Preheat oven: 400° (high)

Sometimes it must seem we're kinky for cheese, we use it in so many recipes. But it is good food and a readily digested source of complete protein.

3 tablespoons unsaturated vegetable oil	½ teaspoon salt
	¾ teaspoon baking soda
¾ cup yoghurt	¼ cup raw wheat germ
¼ pound uncolored, sharp cheddar cheese	1¼ cups whole wheat flour

Mix the oil and yoghurt together in a mixing bowl.

Grate the cheddar cheese into the same bowl. Add the salt and mix.

Mix the baking soda in very well.

Add the wheat germ and flour and mix both in until well distributed.

Grease a baking sheet (see "Greasing without Grease" chapter).

Shape into ¾-inch-thick rounds and bake in preheated oven at about 400° for 20 to 25 minutes.　　　　Yield: 8

7

Custards

Custards are cooked egg puddings, very smooth in texture, and excellent sources of complete protein.

They can be either baked or "boiled." Boiled custards are not literally boiled, but cooked on top of the stove, over boiling water, usually in a double boiler. These are faster to make than baked custards, but not as smooth in texture, and certainly more work, because you have to stir boiled custards constantly while they are cooking.

Baked Custards

Baked custards are made either in one large pot (or pie shell) or in individual custard cups. The same recipe we give for a custard in one large pot can be divided up and cooked in individual cups, but these cups must be baked sitting in water, to distribute the heat. We'll describe that in our first cup custard recipe. Baked in individual servings, the cooking time is, of course, shorter.

We like to use ceramic custard cups. If you have trouble finding these attractive cups, restaurant-supply houses always carry them. Chefs know that ceramic distributes the heat better than metal or oven-proof glass, and it cooks the custard more uniformly. With metal or glass cups, you may find the layer of custard nearer the cup is tougher. Individual cups mean less dishwashing because you serve the custard in them.

You'll see that we use only powdered skim milk for these recipes. Adults should generally use skim milk, but kids need whole milk. If you wish to use certified raw milk, you'll have to scald it for use in these recipes. To scald the milk, heat it slowly to a simmer, then take it from the heat. This kills off the enzymes which tend to fight against the custarding.

For more information on milk and eggs, see the chapter on "Ingredients."

Custard Testing

We usually test all baked custards with a thin metal cake tester, or a shiny metal knife. Both, of course, must be clean. Even done custards may seem uncooked if tested with an unclean tester.

Stick the tester into the center of the pudding and pull it out. If it shows lumps of custard, bake for a while longer. If the tester comes out wet, but free of lumps, the custard is done. If you're not certain, take a spoon and spoon out a bit of one cup. If the custard is done, the hole will stay as dug; if it is not done, there will be some visible running of the liquid egg back into the hole. But understand that this is done only *in extremis:* the custard will never "heal," and you may feel a bit silly bringing a wounded custard to the table.

Do remember that smaller cups cook faster than larger cups. If your cups, like ours, are varied in size and weight, one test may not do for all. But if you test a large cup and it says "done," then your smaller cups are done (how we envy those of you whose custard cups all match).

Warnings for Cup Custards

Be very careful in handling these custard cups, even after they've been out of the oven for a while: the ceramic holds the heat for a long time.

Also, in mixing, don't allow your mixture to get too frothy (as it would if you mixed the ingredients in a blender). A frothy mixture expands in the oven, but then collapses, giving a rather dilapidated looking custard.

BASIC CUP CUSTARD

Preheat oven: 350° to 375°

We will give several flavor variations for this recipe, but there are many more possibilities you can try, once you've got the basic idea down pat.

We use egg yolks in this custard because yolks are better thickeners than whites, but if you don't want so many leftover whites, you can use 3 yolks and 1 whole egg, instead. Or, if you insist, you can use 3 whole eggs instead of the 5 yolks or 3 yolks and 1 whole egg—but you'll have to bake the custard more than 45 minutes. You'll wind up with a custard that's quite tasty and creamy, but without the sturdiness that we like so much in cup custards. If you *do* use 5 yolks, turn to *Angel Food Cake* for what to do with the whites.

Start with hot water for the supermilk* or you may have difficulty getting the honey dissolved and mixed in.

5 large egg yolks, or
  3 large egg yolks and
  1 whole large egg (see
  "Separating Eggs" in
  "Cakes" chapter)

½ cup minus 1 table-
  spoon honey
3 cups supermilk*
1 teaspoon vanilla ex-
  tract

In a large mixing bowl, mix all the ingredients together well. This should yield from 4 to 4½ cups of liquid, depending on how much air there is in the mixture.

Boil about 6 cups of water, and pour into a large shallow pan, such as the bottom of a Dutch oven. You see, cup custards are best cooked with the cups sitting in near-boiling water. The water helps distribute the heat and prevent some scorching and overcooking (overcooking can lead to separation and poor texture).

Divide the custard among about seven cups (our Dutch

*Supermilk: 2½ cups water plus 1 cup noninstant milk powder.

oven holds seven custard cups ranging in capacity from
½ cup to 1 cup), and stand them in the hot water. The
water should come about halfway up the sides of the
cups.

Set the pan in the middle of a preheated oven, and bake
at medium to medium-high temperature for 30 to 35
minutes, or until the custards test done (see "Custard
Testing" earlier in this chapter).

Yield: about 7 servings

COFFEE CUP CUSTARD

1 recipe Basic Cup Custard   *or*
    (*see above*)   *4 level teaspoons*
4 level teaspoons instant   *coffee substitute*
    decaffeinated coffee

Mix and bake as *Basic Cup Custard* (above).

Yield: about 7 servings

MAPLE CUP CUSTARD

5 egg yolks (or 3 yolks plus   *3 cups supermilk*
    1 whole egg—see   *(see* Basic Cup
    "Separating Eggs" in   Custard, *above)*
    "Cakes" chapter)   *1 teaspoon vanilla ex-*
½ cup maple syrup   *tract*

Mix and bake as *Basic Cup Custard* (above).

Yield: about 7 servings

MOCHA CUP CUSTARD

1 recipe Basic Cup Custard   *2 level teaspoons*
    (*see above*)   *instant decaffeinated*
2 level teaspoons carob   *coffee or*
    powder   *coffee substitute*

Mix and bake as *Basic Cup Custard* (above).

Yield: about 7 servings

BANANA CUP CUSTARD

The banana won't stay mixed in this recipe. It floats to the top and forms a soft "crust." Be sure you use the very ripest of bananas.

1½ very ripe bananas   *1 recipe* Basic Cup Custard *(see above)*

Add bananas to *Basic Cup Custard* and fork into a mush.

Bake as *Basic Cup Custard*.

Yield: about 7 large servings

Other Options

You can try almost any flavoring in these custards: for example, almond extract instead of vanilla. Or try ½ cup of shredded desiccated coconut or ground sesame seeds or sunflower seeds.

Try sprinkling the top of each filled cup with nutmeg or cinnamon before baking.

MAPLE-PECAN CUSTARD

Preheat oven: 350° (medium)

Here is a creamy baked custard in the classic style.

We like to bake our large custards in an enamelled iron pot, uncovered. The enamel helps to keep the heat evenly distributed and there is no need for the pan of water that we use with the cup custards.

Don't grease the casserole. Certainly, a bit of custard is apt to stick to the pot, but so what? You serve this custard by spooning it into individual dishes or cups anyhow. The casserole looks handsome when it comes to the table, and you've saved yourself the extra step of greasing and the extra calories.

4 large eggs
1 cup maple syrup
2 cups hot water
⅜ cup noninstant milk powder

1 cup whole wheat bread crumbs
½ cup pecans, coarsely chopped

Break the eggs into the casserole and beat them well for a moment.

Combine the maple syrup, hot water, and milk powder in a shaker or blender and mix well. Add to the eggs in the casserole and mix together.

Add the bread crumbs and mix very well.

In preheated oven, bake at medium temperature for about 25 minutes, or until it tests done. (See "Custard Testing" section earlier in this chapter.)

To serve, spoon custard into individual serving cups and top each serving with a sprinkling of chopped pecans.

Yield: 6 servings

Note:

The bread crumbs form layers at both the top and bottom, so if you can get this custard out with a cake server, you may be able to show off the layers.

CUSTARD PIE FILLING

Preheat oven: 325° to 350°

This can also be served as a large custard, because it doesn't need a crust to be delicious.

To scald raw milk, bring it to a bare simmer in a saucepan, then remove from the heat. Allow to cool before adding it to the eggs.

The raw pie crust must be brushed with a bit of egg white to keep the custard from soaking through. If you wish, add the extra yolk and the leftover white to the custard. It will be all the richer for it. Or, you can use a bit of the white from the recipe. It doesn't take much.

4 large eggs	3 cups made-from-powder
½ cup honey	milk (or 3 cups scalded
	fresh raw milk)
	1 teaspoon vanilla

For Pie

In a large mixing bowl, beat the eggs until well scrambled.

Add the remaining ingredients and mix. Remember, you don't want this mixture to be frothy, or you will get a raised and fallen custard.

Mix and roll your crust for an 8-inch or 9-inch crust as directed in "Pastry" chapter. Brush the inside of the raw crust thinly with egg white.

Pour the raw custard into the pie shell, and bake in a preheated oven, at 325° to 350° for 35 to 40 minutes.

When done, the crust will be lightly browned, and the custard will have a brownish crust. Allow to cool slightly before serving.

For Pudding

To serve as a custard, mix in a large casserole and bake in a preheated 350° oven for about 25 minutes.

COCONUT-CUSTARD PIE FILLING

Preheat oven: 350° (medium)

1 recipe Custard Pie
  Filling *(see above)*

*1 cup desiccated coconut
  shreds*

In a large mixing bowl, mix all ingredients together well.

Bake as *Custard Pie Filling* (see above).

Note:
  Both *Custard Pie Filling* and *Coconut-Custard Pie Filling* also make excellent cup custards.

RICE CUSTARDS

Cooking Short-Grain Brown Rice

For every cup of rice, boil 3 cups of water with about 1 teaspoon of salt (you'll have to taste the result and bring it into line with your own family's likes). When the water is boiling vigorously, add the rice. Reduce heat to low, and give the rice a good stir. Now the water should simmer without boiling over. Cook about 40 to 45 minutes, stirring a few times toward the end of cooking time. As the water gets absorbed, fish out a few grains of rice from time to time and taste them for doneness. Not every variety of rice cooks in the same time.

One cup of dry rice makes 2½ to 3 cups of cooked rice.

While trying to find ideas for cooking rice puddings, we experimented with using milk instead of water, and with putting not-quite-cooked brown rice into the casserole, to complete its cooking. It just didn't work. We cooked brown rice in milk for hours without it getting cooked. So, please, stick to the cooked brown rice for the following recipes.

RICE CUSTARD

⅓ cup noninstant milk powder (or ⅔ cup instant)	½ cup seedless manukka raisins
1⅓ cups cold water	½ teaspoon nutmeg
⅔ cup honey	2½ to 3 cups cooked short-grain brown rice (see "Cooking Short-Grain Brown Rice" earlier in this chapter)
3 large eggs	
rind of ½ orange, grated or finely chopped	
1 teaspoon vanilla extract	

In a large casserole (3 to 4 quarts) mix the milk powder and water together with a whisk.

Add the honey and eggs and beat again until frothy.

Add the remaining ingredients; mix well.

Set casserole in the middle of a cold oven and bake for about 50 minutes at about 350° (medium temperature) or until it tests done (see the beginning of this chapter for "Custard Testing").

Notes:

The orange bits will rise to the top and the raisins and rice will tend to drop to the bottom, so make sure that you serve some of everything in each helping.

Excellent to serve with some supermilk (see Note, *Basic Cup Custard,* page 95) poured over the top.

Yield: 6 servings

Warning:

Make sure your orange peel comes from a California orange, not from a Florida orange which may be dyed.

MAPLE-RICE CUSTARD

4 large eggs	*2 cups cooked short-grain brown rice*
2½ cups warm water	
1 cup instant milk powder	*diced rind of ½ orange*
¾ cup maple syrup	*1 cup seedless manukka raisins*

In a large casserole, whisk the eggs until they are well scrambled.

Add the water, milk powder and maple syrup, and whisk again until thoroughly mixed.

Add the remaining ingredients and stir well.

Put casserole into the middle of a cold oven and bake at about 350° (medium) for 50 to 60 minutes, or until the custard tests done (see "Custard Testing" earlier in this chapter).

Yield: 6 servings

BAKED COCONUT PUDDING

There aren't many eggs in this recipe, so it is only marginally a "custard," but the principles are the same.

3 cups hot water	2 large eggs
¾ cup noninstant milk powder	2 tablespoons unsaturated vegetable oil
1 cup whole wheat bread crumbs	¼ cup honey
1 cup desiccated coconut shreds	rind of ½ lemon, freshly grated

Make up the water and milk powder in a shaker or blender.

Put the bread crumbs and coconut into a 2-quart bowl, pour the milk over them, and allow to stand for 1 hour to absorb and soften.

After 1 hour, break the eggs into an ungreased large casserole, and whisk until well scrambled.

Add the oil, honey, and lemon rind to eggs and whisk again.

Add the milk mixture and stir well.

Starting in a cold oven, bake at about 350° (medium temperature) for about 50 minutes, or until the pudding is well set and the surface is a golden brown.

Yield: 6 servings

Boiled Custards

The trouble with these custards is that you have to stand there and stir them, and then judge when they are done. If they're cooked for too long, they separate. If they're not cooked long enough, they won't thicken. But they are delicious. Besides, baked custards take nearly an hour to make up, while these can go on your table after about 10 minutes cooking.

But don't rely on time with boiled custards.

Testing Boiled Custards

One subjective test is to keep an eye on your stirring

spoon: when the custard begins to form a thick coating on your spoon, it is ready. A more objective test we've used successfully is to keep a candy thermometer (the tubular type) in the top of the double boiler, right in the pudding. A temperature of about 200° is reached at about the time the custard is done.

Good luck.

LOW-FAT BOILED CUSTARD

3 large eggs	⅔ cup instant milk powder
scant ¼ cup honey	½ teaspoon almond extract
1½ cups hot water	

Put up some water to boil in the bottom of a 1-quart double boiler, over high heat.

Put first 4 ingredients into a mixing bowl and beat until smooth and well mixed, then pour mixture into the top of the double boiler. (If you're very neat, you can mix right in the double boiler top, and save washing a bowl. We splash.)

Reduce the heat and cook, stirring constantly for about 10 minutes, or until done. (See "Testing Boiled Custards" just above.)

When cooked, remove from the heat and stir in almond extract.

Serve cool.

Yield: 4 servings

MOCK CHOCOLATE CUSTARD

Please, don't omit the lecithin granules (see "Ingredients" chapter for a discussion of lecithin): they are what make this custard especially creamy.

1½ cups hot water	2 rounded tablespoons
⅔ cup noninstant milk	lecithin granules
powder	3 large eggs
½ cup carob powder	

Put all the ingredients into a blender or shaker and mix very well.

Start the water simmering in the bottom of a double boiler, then pour the mixture into the top of the double boiler.

Stir occasionally until the custard thickens or a candy thermometer reaches 200°.

Serve hot or cold.   Yield: 4 servings

ZABAGLIONE

Here is a dessert made in the grand manner. After dinner, invite your guests into the kitchen and show them how it's done. Altogether (if you have the yolks separated beforehand), it takes only a few minutes.

You can't imagine the taste if you've never had it; we couldn't. But these are for adults only.

Traditional recipes for *Zabaglione* call for *marsala*—an Italian dessert wine. But since we always have a New York State cream sherry on hand, we standardized our recipe on that. Probably any sweet full-bodied dessert wine would make it. Whatever wine you choose, do make sure you like its flavor. You really get the taste of the wine coming through in this recipe, so don't throw in that third-rate "cooking" sherry or you won't like the result. This recipe is worthy of a good wine.

You'll notice that the servings that this recipe yields are quite small, but the flavor is so rich that even this *demitasse* of a serving is quite satisfying.

Now, at last, you know what to do with all those egg yolks left over from making *Angel Food Cake*.

6 *large egg yolks (see*   2 *tablespoons honey*
   "Separating Eggs" section   ¼ *cup cream sherry*
   in "Cakes" chapter)

Put some water up to simmer in the bottom of a double boiler.

In the top of the double boiler (off the stove) mix together the egg yolks and honey, and beat with a wire whisk for about 1 minute.

Put the top of the double boiler over the simmering bottom and drip in the wine, beating all the while. Beat for an additional 2 to 3 minutes until the mixture stands up thick and creamy. The final stage of this thickening comes quite suddenly, so be prepared for it.

Serve hot immediately.   Yield: 4 small servings

COFFEE ZABAGLIONE

If you don't like wine, try this delicious variation.

¼ cup boiling water
2 teaspoons instant decaffeinated coffee or coffee substitute

6 large egg yolks (see "Separating Eggs" in "Cakes" chapter)
2 tablespoons honey

Mix the water and coffee. Then allow coffee to cool enough to put your finger in it.

When cool, proceed as with *Zabaglione* (see above).

Yield: 4 small servings

8

Puddings and Pie Fillings

What you call a pudding depends very much upon your cultural background. If you're Jewish, for example, a pudding may be a potato or noodle concoction that is more a side dish than anything else. If you're British, puddings can be very "suety" things which may taste fine hot, but which greasily stick to the roof of your mouth cold. Last century (or so we've heard), those suety British puddings were a main course, and very adult fare.

If you've grown up within the past ten years or so, a pudding may be something you mix with hot water and stir for an "instant" dessert. Puddings have almost become synonymous with kids, as if adults couldn't enjoy them—probably because those "quick" or "instant" mixes are usually so bland.

This chapter is divided into puddings made with arrowroot starch (see "Ingredients" chapter), and other assorted puddings.

Any arrowroot pudding can be used as a pie filling—and any pie filling as a pudding.

For the fruit puddings, we prefer fresh fruit.

Arrowroot Puddings

Arrowroot starch is fascinating stuff. We describe it in the "Ingredients" chapter, so here we'd just like to repeat a few of the essentials.

Arrowroot acts as does cornstarch: mix it with a liquid and the mixture will thicken when you heat it.

The more arrowroot powder you use, the thicker your pudding will get.

Inventing Your Own

Once you try these recipes and find out how easy and quick it is to make arrowroot puddings in any flavor you wish, you'll never buy an "instant" or packaged pudding again. In fact, you'll be inventing your own puddings.

One tablespoon of arrowroot starch will thicken about 1 cup of liquid, but if the liquid has a lot of solid in it, you won't need as much starch.

If you bring a pudding up to the proper temperature, and the right amount of time has gone by, but it looks as if the pudding isn't going to get thick enough, *don't just throw in a bit more arrowroot*. That won't work. All you'll get is a bunch of white clumps in your finished pudding, and it will be no thicker—and this from a starch which is really much less likely to clump than is corn-starch.

If you find yourself in this hung-up situation, remove the pudding from the heat. Put a tablespoonful of the arrowroot powder into a ¼ cup of hot water and blend it or shake it up until all the powder is dissolved (the liquid will look milky). Then stir the liquid into the pudding and continue to cook.

One great thing about these puddings is that they are fast to cook up. But you do have to stand there and keep stirring them through the cooking, otherwise they will burn.

DATE-MAPLE PUDDING

If you're looking for something that the kids will like and that will still give them good protein, you've arrived: each *helping* has about as much protein and calcium as a pint of milk.

Dates are among the naturally-sweetest of fruits, and the little bit of maple syrup in this recipe probably does more for the flavor than for the sweetness.

We use a blender here, simply because chopping dates can be so messy.

3 cups hot water	⅛ cup maple syrup
1 cup noninstant milk powder	3 tablespoons arrowroot starch
½ pound dates	2 large eggs

Mix the water and milk powder in a blender.

Pit the dates and add them to the milk, blending until they are coarsely ground.

Add the remaining ingredients and blend at low speed until well mixed.

Pour into a 1½- or 2-quart saucepan and cook over medium-low heat, stirring, for about 7 minutes until the pudding thickens. Yield: 4 servings

PINEAPPLE PUDDING

It's simple to make fresh-fruit arrowroot puddings, but the sweetness of the pudding does depend on the sweetness of the fruit. If you're using low-flavor off-season fruit, you may need more sweetener (and even then be a bit disappointed with the taste). However, if you're using very ripe and very sweet fruit, you may want to reduce the amount of sweetener you use. At any rate, do taste the pudding as it cooks: until everything thickens up, it is still not too late to add a bit of sweetener or a bit of extra fruit.

3 cups ripe pineapple chunks	1 cup (additional) pineapple chunks
¼ cup honey	2 tablespoons arrowroot starch

Liquefy the 3 cups of pineapple and honey in a blender.

Blend in the arrowroot at low speed.

Pour into a 1-quart saucepan and add the additional cup of pineapple chunks.

Cook over medium-low heat for 5 to 7 minutes, stirring continuously, until the pudding thickens.

Yield: 4 servings

FRESH ORANGE PUDDING

It takes about 3 medium-sized oranges to make the 2 cups of pulp you'll need. But do not be afraid to experiment with more. Nothing annoys us more than people who try to dictate how our tastes should run—and we believe you've got the same right to make a taste decision.

Really scrub the orange to get the peel clean. Try to get organically-grown oranges, to avoid dyes and insecticides.

2 cups orange pulp	1 seedless orange
1/3 to 1/2 skin of an orange	(additional)
2 tablespoons honey, to taste	2 tablespoons arrowroot starch

Wash, peel, and skin the 3 oranges. Grind or blend the pulp down to a thick juice.

Add the orange peel, diced or finely grated.

Add the honey to your taste: sweeter oranges will need less sweetening.

Blend in the arrowroot starch. Then pour the mixture into a 1-quart saucepan.

Peel the additional orange, cut into chunks, and add to the pan.

Cook over a medium-low flame for 5 to 7 minutes, stirring constantly, until the mixture thickens.

Yield: 4 servings

STRAWBERRY MILK PUDDING

Strawberries have a marvelous flavor—a flavor which begins to diminish as soon as they are removed from the plant. Also, they are an excellent source of vitamin A.

But strawberries are not a very sweet fruit; in fact they are quite tart, even when fully ripe, so don't rely on them to sweeten your recipes.

1½　cups hot water	2½　tablespoons arrowroot
½　cup noninstant milk	starch
powder	2　large eggs
½　cup honey, to taste	2　cups strawberries

Mix the water and milk powder in a shaker or blender.

Add the honey, arrowroot, and eggs. Mix very well.

Add the berries and blend briefly (or mash the berries with a potato masher).

Cook in a 1-quart saucepan, stirring constantly, over medium-low heat until thick: about 7 minutes.

Yield: 4 servings

BANANA PUDDING

Be sure you use only ripe bananas. All bananas are picked and shipped green, but they are not fit to eat until they are soft and have many brown spots—no matter what the ads say.

2　cups warm water	2½　tablespoons arrowroot
½　cup noninstant milk	starch
powder	¼　cup honey
	2　bananas

In a shaker or blender mix the water, milk powder, arrowroot and honey.

If you are using a shaker, coarsely mash the bananas with a fork. For the blender, break the bananas into pieces, then chop coarsely and briefly with the liquid.

Pour mixture into a 1-quart saucepan and cook over medium-low temperature, stirring constantly until thick: 5 to 7 minutes.

Yield: 4 servings

Variation: Banana Mint Pudding

Your home-dried mint will do very well in this recipe.
If you use fresh mint, increase the amount to 2 tablespoons.

1 recipe Banana Pudding   *1 tablespoon dried*
  (see above)   *mint leaves*

Add the mint leaves to the *Banana Pudding* recipe while
still in the blender, then mix and cook as directed.
Yield: 4 servings

MAPLE PUDDING

Maple puddings are what the Madison Avenuers might
refer to as "taste treats." This is a plain pudding, with
high nutritive values (the syrup has valuable mineral
content, and the eggs and milk *are* real eggs and milk),
but you can vary it with a great number of things:
chunks of fruit, chopped nuts, seeds, coconut, and the
like. Don't try it with carob, though, for a chocolate
maple flavor. The carob is sweet on its own and together
they taste terrible.

We do hope, however, that you'll experiment.

2   cups hot water   *3   rounded tablespoons*
⅔ cup noninstant   *arrowroot starch*
  milk powder   *⅝ cup maple syrup, to*
2   large eggs   *taste*

Dump all the ingredients in a blender or shaker. Mix until
smooth.

Taste. If the mixture isn't sweet enough, add some more
syrup. If it's too sweet, add another egg or some more
milk powder. (Did you think you were stuck if it was too
sweet?)

Cook in a 1-quart saucepan, stirring constantly, over
medium-low flame, until the mixture is thick: about 7
minutes.

Yield: 4 servings

COCONUT PUDDING

The amount of sweetener you use in this recipe depends upon your sweet tooth. We tend more toward the bottom of the scale, but then you know your own tastes.

2 cups hot water	½ cup desiccated coconut
2½ rounded tablespoons	shreds
arrowroot starch	½ to 1 cup honey

Mix together the water, arrowroot, coconut, and ½ cup of honey in a blender or shaker, and taste. Add more honey if desired.

Cook in a 1½-quart saucepan, stirring constantly, over medium-low heat, until the pudding thickens: about 5 to 7 minutes.   Yield: 5 to 6 half-cup servings

CREAM PIE FILLING

We're especially fond of this kind of recipe—a "good goody" substitute for an old bad goody.

We use a double boiler here to ensure a smoother texture.

⅜ cup honey	3 level tablespoons
½ cup noninstant milk	arrowroot starch
powder	2 large eggs
1½ cups warm water	1 baked 8-inch pie crust

Mix together until smooth in the top of a double boiler: the honey, milk powder, water, and starch.

Cook over boiling water, stirring constantly, until the mixture begins to thicken.

Remove from the heat and allow to cool slightly.

In another bowl, beat the eggs until very smooth and then stir them into the rest of the mixture.

Put the mixture back over the heat and cook for a few more minutes, stirring constantly, until the mixture thickens.

Cool somewhat and spoon into a baked pie crust.

Yield: one 8-inch pie

BANANA CREAM PIE

1 recipe Cream Pie Filling   *2 ripe bananas*
(see above)

Make up the *Cream Pie Filling*.

When the filling is cooled and in the pie shell, slice the bananas over the set surface.

Yield: one 8- or 9-inch pie

Variation:

For banana flavor *in* the filling, you can blend one additional ripe banana into the honey-milk-water mixture.

CHERRY PIE FILLING

Preheat oven: 400°

We've never had a cherry-pitting machine and pitting cherries is certainly work. Oh well! (See "Ice Cream" chapter for pitting.)

Be certain you use tart pie cherries, not the sweet bing cherries. Pie cherries have much better flavor after cooking.

The odd weight (1¼ pounds) is because this recipe was standardized out of season, on frozen cherries. In season, we'll use 1¼ pounds of the fresh fruit.

1¼ pounds pie cherries	1 egg
½ cup honey	1 uncooked 8-inch pie crust
2 rounded tablespoons arrowroot starch	

Pit the cherries and reserve the juice. (With frozen berries, even the water that has formed as ice we consider to be "juice.")

Pour the juice, honey, and arrowroot starch into a small saucepan.

Cook over a low flame, stirring constantly, until quite thick: about 7 minutes. Then remove from the heat.

Separate the egg (see "Cakes" chapter for "Separating Eggs"). Brush the raw crust with some of beaten white.

Beat the yolk and any leftover white together, then drip into the juice-honey-arrowroot mixture slowly, beating vigorously.

Add the cherries. Cook the whole thing for 1 or 2 minutes more over a low flame, stirring as you do.

Pour mixture into the crust immediately.

Bake at 400° or about 45 minutes, or until the crust has slightly browned.

Allow to cool before serving; the filling will thicken.

Yield: one 8-inch pie

Variation: Quick Cherry Pie

To make a quicker pie with the same ingredients: Prebake your pie shell; put your pitted cherries into the sauce pan along with the juice, honey, and arrowroot. When the pudding is quite thick, simply pour it into the baked shell and allow to cool before serving.

PEACH AND PAPAYA PIE

Preheat oven: 375° to 400°

We use frozen unsweetened organic papaya for this recipe, simply because it's so difficult to get fresh and unsprayed papayas in the North.

If you don't have enough peach and papaya, fill out your measure with wild blueberries.

This pie seems quite exotic when we serve it to friends. The filling stands quite high, and the color combination has to be seen to be believed—especially with the blueberries.

2½ cups of combined   ¾ cup honey
    papaya and peach   3 rounded tablespoons
    chunks   arrowroot starch
1   egg white (see   1 teaspoon dry mint
    "Separating Eggs" in   leaves, rubbed fine
    "Cakes" chapter)   1 unbaked 8- or 9-inch
1½ cups fruit juice   pie crust

Allow the fruit to thaw. Drain off and reserve the juice.
Add enough orange juice to fill out the 1½ cups.

Stir the egg white and brush it on the inside of the crust.

Combine the juice, honey, arrowroot, mint leaves and,
if you wish, any leftover egg in a small saucepan.

Cook over low heat until quite thick. Then remove from
the heat.

Spoon a layer of fruit into the unbaked crust, then a layer
of pudding. Continue alternating fruit and pudding until
used up.

Bake for about 40 minutes. Allow to cool well before
serving.

Yield: one 9-inch pie or a high-crimped 8-inch pie

QUICK PEACH PIE FILLING

Here's a really simple pie, easy and quick to make up,
and quite peachy.

Because we start with a baked pie shell, there's no
need to brush it with any egg white.

1¼ pounds peach slices   5 to 7 tablespoons honey,
1   cup hot water   to taste
3½ tablespoons arrowroot   1 baked 8-inch pie shell
    starch

Combine first 4 ingredients in a large saucepan.

Cook mixture over medium-low heat, until somewhat
thick.

Taste for additional honey, then continue cooking until the pudding is quite thick.

Scrape into the baked pie shell. Allow to cool somewhat before serving.

Yield: one 8-inch pie

Note:

To make this even quicker, forget about the pie shell and eat it as a pudding.

LEMON CREAMPUFFS

This is a triple-threat dessert, because while the recipe is best served in creampuffs, it can also be used as a pie filling, or as a plain, but delicious, pudding.

We use a smooth filling like this to fill the puffs because it must be put into the puffs under a bit of pressure (we'll describe that procedure in detail below) and it's best not to have any lumps in your filling. (That does sound terrible, doesn't it? Lumps in your filling!)

We use fresh lemons and have no idea how one would go about using reconstituted or bottled or frozen lemon juice. There are always fresh lemons in our market and we believe they are available year-round throughout North America.

The pulp of the lemons has food value of its own and also adds a pleasant bit of texture.

For the pastry, see *Sweet Pastry Puffs*, in "Pastry and Pie Crusts" chapter.

2 small lemons	3 tablespoons arrowroot starch
¾ cup honey	
1 cup water	1 baked recipe Sweet Pastry Puffs (see page 129)
2 eggs	

Peel and pit the lemons. Then liquefy the pulp and juice in your blender.

Add the remaining ingredients, except the pastry, to the

blender and mix briefly at low speed until everything is well blended.

Scrape mixture into a 1-quart saucepan.

Cook over medium-low heat for about 5 minutes, stirring constantly until quite thick. Remove from heat.

You could stop now and serve this mixture as a pudding. Or you could use to fill 4 baked tart shells.

To Fill the Puffs

It may sound old fashioned to use a pastry bag (see the chapter on "Icings") for this kind of work, but we do and we recommend it highly.

Take a nozzle that you never use, and with a screwdriver, pry the nozzle open wider so that it has an opening of about ¼ inch. The opening of the nozzle should be small enough to keep the filling in, but wide enough to allow it easy exit when you squeeze the bag. Wash the nozzle and screw it into your clean pastry bag.

Spoon enough of the filling into the bag to fill it about halfway. Don't overfill your bag because the pudding will back up on you and spill out the top of the bag all over your shoes (or all over your feet, if you cook barefooted).

Without squeezing, gently fold the top of the bag together, preparatory to squeezing.

Pick up an empty puff, poke the nozzle into its side, and gently squeeze the bag. The amount you squeeze in depends on how full you like your creampuffs. That's all there is to it.

Yield: 18 to 24 puffs

Note:

Be sure you wash the bag and nozzle well before you put it away.

LEMON PIE FILLING

You need a bit more filling for a pie than for cream-puffs.

4 *small lemons*	*4½ tablespoons arrowroot*
1½ cups honey	* starch*
2 cups water	*1 baked 8-inch pie shell*
3 large eggs	

Follow directions for making the filling in *Lemon Creampuffs* (see above), but pour mixture into the pie shell instead of puffs.

Yield: one 8-inch pie

LEMON PUDDING

Follow the recipe for *Lemon Creampuffs* (see above), but reduce the arrowroot starch to 2 tablespoons. (You won't need the puff shells either.)

If you follow the proportions in the *Lemon Pie Filling* recipe (see above), use only 3½ tablespoons of arrowroot.

Yield: 4 servings

Assorted Puddings

Here we go into miscellaneous puddings. These are especially for those of you who prefer not to use any thickeners at all.

APPLE PIE FILLING

Preheat oven: 350°

This really is a classic: rather tart and *very* apple.

For an 8-inch pie, use 1½ pounds of apples; for a 9-inch pie, use 2 pounds of apples.

1½ or 2 pounds fresh,   ½   teaspoon cinnamon
   tart apples   1   tablespoon fresh lemon
¼ teaspoon salt   juice
1 tablespoon honey

a bit of egg white (see "Separating Eggs" in "Cakes" chapter)
1 unbaked, 8- or 9-inch pie crust

Wash and core the apples, but do not peel. Cut into slices
less than ¼-inch thick.

Pour the salt, honey, cinnamon and lemon juice over the
apple slices and stir repeatedly, until well coated. Taste
for additional spice or honey (but do avoid adding too
much honey—you rather spoil the effect if the pie comes
out sweet).

Brush the inside of the pie crust with some egg white.

Pile the slices high inside the crust (they will tend to
settle somewhat during baking).

In your preheated oven, bake at 375° to 400° for 45 to
50 minutes or until the apple slices are tender and the
crust begins to brown.

Yield: one 8- or 9-inch pie

QUICK APPLE PIE FILLING

Here's another "quick" filling—one that's cooked
separately from the crust. The pies or tarts made this
way do come out very crisp. And it's easier to tell whether
or not the filling wants some flavor adjustment.

2½ pounds tart apples   2   teaspoons cinnamon
1 small lemon (with skin)   1   teaspoon cloves
½ cup honey

1 baked 9-inch pie shell; or 6 baked 4-inch tart shells

Wash and core the apples, but do not peel. Cut into cubes.

Wash the lemon well and pit it, but do not peel it. Slice
into very thin shavings and add to the apple cubes.

Add the remaining ingredients, except pastry shells, and mix well.

Cook in a large pot over medium heat for about 10 minutes, or until the apples have softened but still retain some body.

Spoon into baked pie shell or tart shells and serve.

Yield: one 9-inch pie; or six 4-inch tarts

PEACH MOUSSE

Here, again, you'll want to chill your mixing bowl and beaters before you begin to whip. You may whip all day in a warm bowl and never get anything near whipped.

This may look like a complicated recipe (lots of ingredients), but it isn't difficult.

1 cup ice water	½ cup water (additional)
1 cup noninstant milk powder	¼ cup honey
½ teaspoon almond extract	1¼ cups peach chunks (enough for 1 cup of mush when mashed)
1 teaspoon unflavored gelatin	⅜ cup honey (additional)

Pour the ice water and milk powder into a large chilled mixing bowl.

Beat at medium-high speed until the mixture begins to thicken. Then add the almond extract and continue to beat until very thick—15 to 20 minutes total.

In a small saucepan, dissolve the gelatin in the ½ cup of water. Add the ¼ cup of honey and mix.

Heat, stirring, until the mixture clears. Remove from heat and cool (but don't allow it to get so cool that it sets).

In another bowl, mash up the peach chunks with ⅜ cup of honey.

Beat the gel mixture into the whipped milk powder. Mix in the peach mixture.

Serve as is, or put into the refrigerator to set further, or into the freezer to solidify. Each way works and results in a pleasant texture.

Yield: 6 servings

INDIAN PUDDING

This is a traditional American dish. It contains cornmeal and molasses, both very Colonial ingredients.

Since this recipe is set as much by the cornmeal as by the eggs, feel free to use whole milk, even if raw—neither will keep the pudding from setting.

We make this recipe with both Barbados and blackstrap molasses because some people find the blackstrap molasses too strong and not sweet enough. If you're a blackstrap freak already, substitute an additional ⅓ cup of the blackstrap for the ½ cup of Barbados.

4 cups hot water		
1½ cups instant milk powder	} or 4 cups whole milk	
2 tablespoons unsaturated vegetable oil	⅓ cup blackstrap molasses	
¾ teaspoon salt	2 large eggs	
½ cup Barbados molasses	1 teaspoon cinnamon	
	1 cup freshly-ground cornmeal	

In a shaker or in a blender, mix the water, milk powder, oil, salt and all of the molasses.

In an ungreased, 3- or 4-quart casserole, beat the eggs until frothy.

Add the blender mixture to the eggs and stir well.

Add the cinnamon and cornmeal and stir in well.

Bake in a medium oven (about 350°) for about 1 hour or until set.

Especially good served with some *Whipped Topping* (see "Miscellany" chapter) or cold milk.

Yield: 8 servings

RICE CREAM

Here's a frothy and creamy pudding that both kids and adults will go for (if they like frothy, creamy puddings).

1 cup cooked brown rice (see "Cooking Short-Grain Brown Rice" in "Custards" chapter)	2 large egg yolks (see "Separating Eggs" in "Cakes" chapter)
2 cups warm water	½ cup honey
⅔ cup instant milk powder	2 large egg whites

In the top of a large double boiler, combine the rice, water, and milk powder. Warm over moderate heat.

In a large bowl, beat together the egg yolks and honey until frothy.

Add to the warmed mixture in the top of the double boiler. Mix well, and allow to cook about ½ hour until somewhat thick. Cool.

In a large mixing bowl, beat the egg whites until very stiff.

Add the cooled rice mixture and beat all together until smooth.

The texture is that of a thick bisque, but if you insist on something firmer, you can turn this mixture into a mousse by setting it in the freezer in individual cups for a few hours.

Yield: 4 servings

HADASSAH'S KUGEL

Kugel is Yiddish for pudding, so you see we haven't really changed the subject.

This recipe (of course we adapted it—we always adapt) was given to us by a dear friend, who adapted it from a recipe of her mother's. We don't know where her mother got it, but she was serving it 60 years ago in Turkey.

Kugels are rather heavy for a dessert, usually they are served as a side dish with the meat course of a dinner. This *kugel* is different, sweet and chewy, but the first and second versions would also make excellent side dishes.

We use artichoke noodles (American or Jerusalem artichokes, not the thistle kind), but you could just as well use broad whole wheat noodles or spinach noodles. And don't overcook them. Artichoke and whole wheat noodles cook up faster than commercial white noodles.

I

½ pound broad artichoke
  noodles, cooked al dente
¼ cup blackstrap molasses
⅜ cup Barbados
  molasses
¼ cup boiling water

3 large eggs
3 heaping tablespoons
  raw wheat germ
½ teaspoon salt
1 teaspoon vanilla extract
1 teaspoon dried basil

Allow the cooked noodles to drain well.

Meanwhile, combine all of the molasses in a large skillet. Cook over a medium-low heat until the mixture bubbles and the bubbles cover the entire surface.

Add the boiling water. Stir in, and remove skillet from heat.

Scrape the cooked noodles into the skillet and stir.

Beat the eggs. Add to the skillet and stir.

Add the wheat germ, salt, vanilla, and basil, and stir until well mixed.

Grease a straight-sided casserole (see "Greasing without Grease" chapter). Pour mixture in but don't stir.

Starting cold, bake in a medium oven (350°) for about 30 minutes, or until the top is crisp.

Remove from the oven, (carefully), cover with the business side of a large round platter, and turn upside down.

The pudding should come out in one piece and look like a rather strange, low cake. If you've greased with oil or if you've greased poorly, the *kugel* will stick and break up. No real harm done. The crisp parts are still crisp and the flavor is still great.

Yield: 4 to 8 servings (Depends on whether you use it as a dessert, side dish, or as a vegetarian main course.)

II

Here's a bigger and sweeter version, with more protein.

½ pound broad artichoke
noodles, cooked al dente
¼ cup blackstrap molasses
⅜ cup Barbados molasses
¼ cup boiling water
4 large eggs
3 heaping tablespoons
raw wheat germ

½ teaspoon salt
1 teaspoon vanilla extract
2 teaspoons dried basil
2 large, sweet apples
1 cup manukka raisins

Follow directions for *Hadassah's Kugel I* (above). The fruit gets stirred in gently after the *kugel* is poured into the casserole.

Yield: 6 to 8 servings

9

Pastry and Pie Crusts

"Pastry" is a word to conjure with. It evokes images of the whitest white flour and the most saturated butter (and the hardest arteries).

But, it doesn't have to be that way. You can come up with the lightest, flakiest, tastiest pastries imaginable, with whole wheat pastry flour and unsaturated liquid vegetable oil.

Yes, you can have eclairs, creampuffs, baked donuts, even very-cakelike pastries—all with only healthy ingredients. You'll never believe how good these can be until you try them yourself.

Puff Pastry

Read the instructions for *Whole Wheat Puffs* because we'll use the same techniques for all the puff pastry recipes.

Be sure you do preheat your oven—these won't work in a cold oven—and that you beat the eggs in very well. Also, be sure that you allow the batter to cool only enough to keep the eggs from cooking when you break them in.

WHOLE WHEAT PUFFS

Preheat oven: 450° (high)

Let's start out with this modestly-puffed dish. It is usable as a hot hors d'oeuvre or even as a dessert puff.

1 cup water
⅛ teaspoon salt
½ cup unsaturated
  vegetable oil

1 cup whole wheat
  flour
3 large eggs

Boil the water and salt in a 4-quart pot.

Add the oil, stir, and allow to come to a boil again.

Reduce the heat to low and dump in all the flour at once.

Begin to stir immediately, and stir briskly for a minute or two, until the mixture pulls away from the sides of the pot. (It will look like cooked oatmeal.)

Remove from the heat and continue to stir briskly for another minute.

Allow to cool for a few minutes. You are about to add eggs, and you don't want the mixture to be hot enough to cook them. But you don't want to let it get cold, either.

Break an egg into the mixture and beat the mixture with a fork until the egg is very well mixed in.

Beat in another egg.

Beat in the third egg and continue to beat until the mixture takes on a *shiny* look.

Grease 2 large baking sheets (see "Greasing without Grease" chapter) and spoon out teaspoonfuls of the batter, leaving a bit of spreading room between each.

When batter is all spooned, use your fingers to gently smooth out any peaks.

Bake in preheated oven, at about 450°, until the peaks begin to brown (15 to 20 minutes) then reduce the heat to 350° (medium) and continue to bake for another 10 to 15 minutes or until firm. Then remove from the oven.

Yield: about 45 puffs

Note:

You can eat these as they are, or cut off the tops and spoon in some kind of filling. For example, try the *Fish Filling* (see "Miscellany" chapter). Or split and eat with *Tomato Jam* (see "Jams and Jellies").

SWEET PASTRY PUFFS

Preheat oven: 450° (high)

This is the basic pastry recipe for things like *Eclairs, Jelly Donuts, Creampuffs,* and *Donuts.*

We use whole wheat *pastry* flour instead of all-purpose whole wheat flour here; the finer grind and softer wheat make it better suited for the desserty pastries. The additional egg makes for additional rise.

1 cup water	*1 cup whole wheat*
½ cup unsaturated	*pastry flour*
vegetable oil	*4 large eggs*
¼ teaspoon salt	*1 teaspoon vanilla extract*

Measure the water, oil, and salt into a 4-quart pot and bring to the boil.

Add all the flour at once, and immediately begin to stir batter briskly with a fork, until it is quite cohesive, and the texture of well-cooked oatmeal.

Remove from the heat and allow to cool for 5 minutes.

One at a time, beat the eggs in very well with a fork, until the batter shows a satiny sheen.

Stir the vanilla in well.

Grease 2 large baking sheets (see "Greasing without Grease" chapter), and spoon out tablespoonfuls of the batter, leaving room for it to rise and spread.

Bake as described in *Whole Wheat Puffs* (see above), but add about 5 to 10 additional minutes baking time. The Puffs must come out rather firm, but unburnt.

Yield: about 16 large puffs

Note:

When done and firm, cut off the tops for filling with *Creme Chantilly* (see "Miscellany" chapter), or fill with a pudding (see *Lemon Pudding* in "Puddings and Pie Fillings" chapter) for a *Creampuff* or *Jelly Donuts*, as described on page 118.

ECLAIRS

A pastry bag is necessary for *Eclairs* and for the *Creampuffs, Jelly Donuts*, and *Donuts* which follow, so if you plan to try these pastries, by all means make the $2.00 investment.

A pastry bag is made of a lined canvas cloth formed into a cone. At one end it is open wide, and at the narrow end it is fitted with a threaded tube for the attachment of various icing nozzles. You know, those things to make swirls and stars and things with *Maple Butter Icing* (see "Icings and Cake Fillings" chapter). For the recipes in this section you don't need the special shapes. In fact, for *Eclairs* you don't even need a nozzle; you can use the bag without any of the attachments. Fold up the nozzle and the narrowest bit of cloth to keep the batter from dripping out before you're ready.

Don't fill the bag more than halfway. If you do, the batter will back up and come gushing out over your feet. We've learned that from messy experience.

After you've spooned batter into the bag (it should take no more than two fillings to finish the batter), twist the top closed and allow a thick line of batter about 4 inches long to ooze onto a greased baking sheet (see chapter on "Greasing without Grease"). You'll need 2 baking sheets.

Leave room for rising and spreading.

When you're fiinished with the pastry bag, be sure you soak and wash it quickly. Well-hardened pastry is murder to get off.

Let's get to the recipe.

Preheat oven: 450° (high)

1 *recipe* Sweet Pastry Puffs   ½ *recipe* Cooked Honey
  (see above)   Icing *(see page 172)*
1 *recipe* Creme Chantilly
  (see page 210)

Mix the batter together, fill the pastry bag with it and squeeze out the raw *Eclair* shapes as described earlier in this recipe.

Bake as described for *Whole Wheat Puffs* (see above) until golden and quite firm.

When baked, remove *Eclairs* from oven and allow to cool slightly. If you've baked them firm enough, there should be no falling.

When cool, slice in half, horizontally, and spoon some *Creme Chantilly* onto each bottom piece.

Replace the tops, and drip a bit of *Cooked Honey Icing* over it.

Serve at once, or chill before serving. Once filled, these won't keep long. Within a few hours, the filling will make the pastry a bit soggy.

Yield: about 18 eclairs

Variation:

You can fill the *Eclairs* with a combination of *Creme Chantilly* and any of our jams (except *Tomato Jam*). Or you can fill them with *Creme Chantilly* mixed with diced strawberries and chilled. Or fill them with just a bit of jam, without any *Creme* at all.

DONUTS

Preheat oven: 375° to 400°

Real donuts are deep fried, and there are few pastries that are worse for you. The very high temperature of the fat tends to saturate the donuts. Stay away from them.

In this recipe, we use the puffy nature of the *Sweet*

Pastry dough to get baked rings which we call "donuts" because they look like them. They are puffed, not cake-like, but they are wholesome, delicious, and light.

1 recipe Sweet Pastry Puffs *(above)*	*½ recipe* Cooked Honey Icing *(optional) (see page 172)*

Prepare your pastry dough as described in *Sweet Pastry Puffs*.

Spoon into a pastry bag, as described in *Eclairs* (above).

Using 2 greased baking sheets (see "Greasing without Grease" chapter), squeeze the batter into individual circles, about 3 inches in diameter. Be certain you leave a hole in the middle, about 1 inch wide.

Bake in preheated oven (375° to 400°) for about 40 minutes, or until well risen, golden colored, and firm.

Remove from the oven, cool, and if you like top with drippings of *Cooked Honey Icing*. Or eat as they come from the oven, still warm.

Yield: about 16 donuts

CREAMPUFFS/JELLY DONUTS

For our purposes, there is no difference between *Creampuffs* and *Jelly Donuts*, except their filling.

Creampuffs should be filled with something like *Creme Chantilly* (see page 210), or *Whipped Topping* (page 211). *Jelly Donuts* are filled with any of the pudding recipes made with arrowroot starch (see "Other Puddings" in the "Puddings and Pie Fillings" chapter).

Your pastry bag comes into play again, here. The fillings have to be "pumped" into the pastry hole, and this is done with a pastry bag, fitted this time with a nozzle.

Our pastry bag did not come fitted with a large-aperture nozzle. If yours did, you have no problem. We wound up taking a screwdriver and prying open one of the nozzles to make a hole roughly ¼-inch across.

Once the nozzle is on and the bag filled (with the nozzle on, the filling is unlikely to drip out), poke the nozzle into the side of the *Puff*, and squeeze in as much filling as desired. The amount of filling you use is much a matter of taste. However, with too much filling, the *Puff* soon gets soggy.

To make *Creampuffs* or *Jelly Donuts* you need:

1 recipe Sweet Pastry Puffs   *1 recipe filling of your*
(see above)   *choice*

Make up and bake as described for *Sweet Pastry Puffs*.

Fill as described above, and serve immediately.

Yield: 16 large puffs or donuts

Note:

We especially recommend *Lemon Pudding* (see page 119).

Pie Crusts

We spent years thinking that pie crusts were bad food because they had to be made with hard fat and white flour. It isn't so. They can be made successfully, flakily, and deliciously, with oil. They don't have to be made of grain flour at all. We make them successfully with nut or seed flours (though these are more difficult to handle than the wheat crusts).

All of the pie crust recipes that follow are for single-crust pies. We don't make any other kind. One crust has enough calories for us. Most recipes yield a 9-inch crust, or an 8-inch crust with a high crimped edge (we'll describe that below).

Making the Crust

Measure the flour and salt into a medium-sized mixing bowl and mix them together.

Drip in the oil a bit at a time, and mix well with a

fork after each dripping. You know you have enough oil when the mixture looks like a bowlful of large crumbs.

Add ice water, 1 tablespoon at a time, mixing very well between tablespoonfuls. When the dough forms easily into a cohesive and firm ball, you've added enough water.

Lay out a large piece of waxed paper and place the ball on it. Press with your hand to flatten it slightly. Place another piece of waxed paper over the flattened ball, and roll out, into a circle $3/16$ of an inch thick. If the edges crack badly and the dough is obviously not holding together, gather it up, return it to the bowl, and add another tablespoon of ice water, then roll it out again.

To save time for your next pie, keep track of how much water and oil you use with what kind of flour. Amounts may vary from flour to flour.

Tarts

Tarts get rolled a bit thinner to start with—say ⅛ inch. Any of these recipes should make six 4-inch tarts.

We don't recommend the nut or seed crusts for tarts. They don't roll as thin or handle as easily.

Panning

Once the crust is rolled between waxed paper, grease an 8- or 9-inch pie pan (see the chapter on "Greasing without Grease"), lift off the top layer of waxed paper, and smoothly and gently reverse the crust and remaining paper over the pie pan. Remove the second paper gently.

By gently lifting and even more gently pressing, shape the crust to the pan. If tears appear, just press the dough to close them, or pick off bits of dough from the outside edges and press them over the tears.

There will be dough left over (at least there should be, if you've rolled it thin enough), and you can either cut it off, or crimp it.

Crimping

Basically, crimping is just pinching the dough between your fingers so that it stands up higher than the rim of the pan. If you have any skill in it (like Floss does), you can get a lovely wavy effect. If your skills are more on Stan's level, then it may wind up looking like a drunkard's dream. Either way or in between, you can improve your technique by practice.

Baking

Most often, the shells are baked with the filling, but for separate baking times, see the individual recipes.

Pricking

If you prebake a pie shell, you can come up against a problem you don't find when baking shell and filling together. The bottom may buckle. To prevent this, prick the bottom of the crust with a fork in a dozen or so places.

WHOLE WHEAT PASTRY PIE CRUST

Preheat oven: 375° (medium-high)

This is the finest of our crusts, with a texture every bit as good as what you can get with hard fat and white flour.

When you roll out your crust, do try to make it even, and in as round a circle as you can manage. Remember, there is no law that says that if you aren't satisfied with a rolling, that you have to go ahead and bake it anyhow. If you don't like the thickness or the shape, pick the crust off the waxed paper, reshape it into a ball, and roll all over again.

Someday, you may be able to roll out a perfect crust in 3 minutes, but *not* the first time you try. Meanwhile it's a fun thing to do.

1½ cups whole wheat pastry   ¼   teaspoon salt
    flour   3 to 4 tablespoons ice water
⅓   cup unsaturated
    vegetable oil

Mix, roll, and put dough into a pie pan as described just
above.

To bake the empty shell, set in a 375° preheated oven for
10 to 15 minutes, or until brown and firm.

Yield: one 8- or 9-inch shell

WHOLE WHEAT AND WHEAT GERM CRUST

Preheat oven: 375° (medium-high)

1¼ cups whole wheat flour   ⅓   cup unsaturated
¼   cup raw wheat germ   vegetable oil
                               ¼   teaspoon salt
                               3   tablespoons ice water

Mix, roll, and pan as described in the beginning of this
section.

To bake just the shell, bake in a preheated medium-high
oven for about 12 minutes, or until brown.

Yield: one 8- or 9-inch pie shell

WHOLE WHEAT AND NUT CRUST

Preheat oven: 375° (medium-high)

The combination of flour and ground nuts is especially
tasty in this recipe, which yields enough for two crusts.

½   cup filberts, shelled   ⅓   cup unsaturated
1½ cups whole wheat   vegetable oil
    pastry flour   ¼   teaspoon salt
                               2 to 3 tablespoons ice water

In a blender or grinder, grind the filberts into a fine flour.
Put the nut flour in a mixing bowl.

Add the whole wheat flour and mix well.

Mix, roll, and pan as described in the beginning of this section.

To prebake, put in a preheated medium-high oven for about 12 minutes. Yield: *two* 8-inch pie crusts

WHOLE WHEAT SESAME CRUST

Preheat oven: 375° (medium-high)

Sesame seeds add a marvelous flavor to the whole wheat. We use less oil and more water with this recipe, making it a bit lower in calories than the others.

1¼ cups whole wheat pastry flour	¼ cup unsaturated vegetable oil
¼ teaspoon salt	5 tablespoons ice water
¼ cup unhulled sesame seeds	

Mix, roll, and pan as described in the beginning of this section.

To prebake, put crust in preheated oven and bake at medium-high for about 15 minutes, or until firm and browning.

Yield: one 8-inch crust

SUNFLOWER-SEED CRUST

Seeds and nuts make delicious pie crusts, but they don't handle as easily as wheat crusts, or crusts made with a combination of seeds and wheat. This recipe must be rolled thicker than the grain crusts, and it is still apt to crack. Cracking isn't a real problem, however. Just get the crust into the pan, as best you can, and repair any cracks with the extra dough or by pressing the cracks closed.

Don't worry about the thickness of the crust. It still comes out quite light.

2 cups hulled sunflower seeds	⅓ cup unsaturated vegetable oil
	2 tablespoons ice water

In a blender or grinder, grind the sunflower seeds to a fine flour (yields about 2½ cups ground).

Mix, roll, and pan as described in the beginning of this section.

To bake the crust, start in a cold oven and bake for about 30 minutes at about 350° (medium) until brown.

Yield: one 8-inch crust

COOKIE CRUST

Preheat oven: 350° (medium)

As the name states, this crust is made with cookies, ground and mixed with oil, then pressed into the pie pan. In case you wonder which kinds of cookies make the best crusts, we can only tell you that any plain cookie, not burnt, will do. We used the failures from our "Cookies" chapter: the ones without good enough flavor to make it into the book. If you have no failures, you're just going to have to use good cookies.

1¼ cups cookie crumbs	2 tablespoons
¼ cup unsaturated vegetable oil	ice water

Grind your cookies in a blender (or pound them fine with a mortar and pestle), and pour into a large mixing bowl.

Add the oil a bit at a time, mixing well with a fork, until the cookie flour forms into largish clumps.

Add the water, 1 tablespoon at a time, squeezing the mixture together well after each tablespoon. You want to have it a cohesive ball. You may want to add a bit more water if it won't cohere well.

Tear off bits of the dough and press by thumb, evenly, into an *ungreased*, 8-inch pan, until you have it in a crust shape.

Fork a dozen or so holes into the bottom of the crust to prevent warping.

Bake at medium in a preheated oven for about 10 minutes.

Yield: one 8- or 9-inch pie crust

APPLE TAKE ALONGS

You've seen miniature pies in the market? The ones you can just stick into a lunchbox or brown bag to take along to school or work?

Well, these aren't quite the same—they're much better. These *Take Alongs* have more filling, without the chemicals, and a thinner and healthier crust. And they taste delicious.

The thinner crust must be handled more carefully than most crusts.

Filling	Crust
2 large apples	1 recipe Whole Wheat
¼ teaspoon cinnamon	Pastry Pie Crust (above)
1 teaspoon fresh lemon juice	
1 teaspoon honey	

Wash the apples well; core but do not peel them. Chop them quite small, and put in a large mixing bowl. Add the remaining ingredients, and mix very well. Allow to stand.

Mix the pie crust as described in the beginning of this section.

Form into a rough ball. Place ball on a large piece of waxed paper. Press somewhat flat with your hand, cover with another piece of waxed paper, and roll flat with a rolling pin. (You want to roll this crust somewhat thinner than a normal crust.)

Remove the top paper, and cut the pastry into 4 equal pieces.

Spoon a quarter of the mixture onto half of each piece

of pastry and gently and carefully work the other half up and over, pinching it closed where it comes together. Don't struggle for any particular shape of *Take Along*. Just get that crust up and over the filling in the neatest shape you can. And don't worry if a little apple shows— that doesn't matter at all.

Place on a greased baking sheet (see "Greasing without Grease" chapter) and bake, starting in a cold oven, for 45 to 50 minutes at 375° to 400°.

Yield: 4 take alongs

Note: Serve hot, or pack into a lunchbox to take along.

DATE BARS (Spoon Pastry)

Here's a pastry that's quite different, because you don't roll the dough out, but rather press it into place with the back of a spoon.

You can make a filling for spoon pastry with any dried fruit, cut and mashed to a thick paste. We use dates because they mash up so easily.

Crust

⅓ cup unsaturated
    vegetable oil
⅓ cup honey
1   cup rolled oats
1½ cups whole wheat
    pastry flour
    (approximate)

Filling

½ pound dates (weighed
    with pits in)
½ cup water

In a large mixing bowl, mix together the oil, honey, and oats. Add enough of the flour to make a mixture that will *almost* form into a cohesive ball.

Pit and quarter the dates, and put them into a medium-sized saucepan with the water.

Cook over gentle heat, mashing dates with a potato masher until you get a thick paste. Remove from the heat.

Grease an 8-inch square cake pan (see chapter on "Greasing without Grease"), and spoon in half the *dough*, pressing it into a cohesive, roughly-flat sheet with the back of a large spoon (it will look like a solid crust).

With a rubber spatula, spread all the *filling* over this crust. Be gentle, too rough handling and you'll poke through the crust.

Scrape on the rest of the pastry mixture, spread it, and, again, with the back of a large spoon, press *gently*, uniformly, into place over the date paste.

With a very sharp knife, cut the raw pastry into 2-inch squares.

Starting in an unheated oven, bake at about 350° (medium) for 20 to 25 minutes, or until the top begins to brown.

Turn out and serve when cool.   Yield: 16 two-inch bars

10

Cakes

There is almost as much mythology built up about cakes as there is about bread. You must tiptoe through the kitchen or the cake will fall; you must never open the oven door until you're certain the cake is almost done; you must never slam the oven door or the cake will collapse . . . our oven door won't stay closed unless we slam it, and we never tiptoe except in a hospital, and we like to peek.

Yet, despite all this, we have great success with cakes. Cakes are easy. They are so easy, it's amazing that the cake-mix industry ever sprang up at all. They are not delicate. They are a snap to make with whole wheat flour, honey and yoghurt (and other "difficult" ingredients). And they make up so quickly that we can't imagine how anyone can think they're saving time with a mix.

Sifting

Don't. We never sift our pastry flour. The only concession we make to clumps is to break them up with a fork when they appear.

Chemicals

We generally use baking soda to make our cakes rise (bicarbonate of soda is the same thing). This is an alkalizing agent, and a natural product. Which doesn't mean we recommend it without reservation (poison hemlock is natural, too). The body chemistry should run slightly acid; too much alkalizing is bad for you, it throws your chemical balance off. So we never recommend or use large amounts of bicarb.

What we do use is a teaspoon or so at a time, and we include something acid to neutralize this, usually a half or even a full cup of yoghurt. It's better to have a little acid left over than alkali.

What happens is that when the soda (the alkali) and the yoghurt (the acid) come together, they neutralize one another, and in this chemical reaction, bubbles are released. These bubbles expand in the heat of baking, and that's how the cake rises.

We have found that the use of this small amount of soda in combination with the yoghurt gives you enough rise. The yoghurt also gives you a marvelously light texture, like sour cream. (Sour cream or any cultured milk —buttermilk or sour milk—can be substituted for the yoghurt.)

Most standard recipes for cakes call for both baking soda and baking *powder*. Now, let us do a number on baking powder. It usually contains aluminum as well as other chemical ingredients (there is nonaluminum powder on the market, but it has other undesirable chemicals in it).

There is no need for baking powder when the very cheap baking soda will give you the same results, if you know how to use it.

Cake Pans and Cake Sizes

Don't bake our cakes in larger pans than we call for or they will not rise adequately. If you bake in pans smaller than called for, use more pans and don't fill them more than ⅔ full.

If you want to increase the recipe, again, use more pans, not bigger ones.

We are really very fond of cakes in shaped pans:

Turk's head, sand torte, banana swirls, tube pan, ring mold. The hole in the middle makes for faster baking and makes it easier for the batter to rise evenly because the batter clings to something in the center as well as on the outside. But, if you leave a spot ungreased, getting your cake out of these shaped molds can be a disaster.

However, most of the recipes we give can be baked as layer cakes as well as in the shaped pans we recommend. The important thing is to keep the volumes of the pans in mind. If a recipe calls for a 6-inch Turk's head pan, you can most likely bake it in a layer pan, but before you try, check the volumes of both pans. If the Turk's head holds more (just pour water from one to the other to find out), you're very likely to overflow the layer pan.

Angel Food and *Cranberry Cake*, however, are two recipes that should not be put in layer pans.

Moisture

We've never had trouble getting moist cakes. Starting out with the right ingredients and baking for an appropriate time in the right temperature slot should give you a moist cake.

You do not get a moist cake by starting with a very wet batter. Batter that is too wet can be scorched on the outside and still raw on the inside. Or, if you bake it in a very slow oven, the same cake may turn out done in the middle, but quite hard and dry near the outside.

By all means experiment, but, if your batter is very liquid, you have a good chance of failure. Start out by following a recipe closely. If the cake turns out to your satisfaction, keep a note of how moist the batter was. When you experiment you can then aim for the same wetness.

We do find that yoghurt helps a good deal in keeping cakes moist, and honey is a natural holder of moisture (honey will even absorb humidity from the air).

On of the most spectacular failures we had in inventing and standardizing these recipes was a too-liquid batter.

The batter rose right out of the pan and all over the oven. Messy, messy.

Separating Eggs

There are a number of ways you can separate the whites and yolks of eggs. There are even utensils sold for this purpose. If you know a method, you don't need to read the following paragraphs. However, if you've never separated eggs, read on.

Remember, what you want to do is make certain that no yolk get in with the white. If it does, the white may not whip up stiff. But it doesn't matter if you get a little white in with the yolk.

Your first chance for failure comes with cracking the egg. We've done it many times—hit the egg too hard and had the yolk break, or hit the egg too gently and then had to mangle it open, and again broke the yolk. You want the egg to open the first try, and you want to be able to separate the two halves cleanly.

After hitting the egg against a firm surface, hold the egg with either end down over the bowl in which you're going to beat the white. As you lift off the top half of the egg, some of the white will plop right into the bowl.

Now, holding the empty half of the egg shell close to the full half, and being very careful not to drop the yolk into the bowl, pour the yolk into the other half (allowing some more white to drip into the bowl). This should get most of the white into its bowl. You can repeat the maneuver once more to get the rest of the loose white, and then drop the yolk into another bowl (or jar for refrigerating—they go bad quickly if not used).

There is still a bit of white clinging to the inside of the shell halves, so pick up one half and, using your finger, scrape out what white you can. Repeat with the other half. This may sound troublesome, but with the price of eggs what it is, you want every bit of white you've paid for.

Greasing

For all these recipes, except *Angel Food*, grease your pan according to our "Greasing without Grease" chapter.

Testing Cakes for Doneness

It's not hard, really. (Though it's not as easy as winding your watch, either.) We use two different objects for testing cakes. First of all, we use a "cake tester" for use during the baking. This is a wire some 8 inches long, about the gauge of a heavy needle, with a loop in the top to make it easy to handle. It is steel, so it won't rust. In the old days people used a clean broom straw for this purpose. We have never had a clean broom; we bought this wire for ten cents in a hardware store about ten years ago.

We stick the tester into the top of the cake, all or most of the way through. If the wire comes out with *batter* sticking to it, there's no question that more baking is required (if, at this time, the outside already looks as if it's scorching, reduce the heat to as low as you can make it, or shut it off entirely; sometimes a cake that's almost done will finish in a hot, turned-off, oven).

If, however, the wire comes out clean, we don't assume "Done," and whisk it onto the table. That wire is a preliminary indicator, not an infallible gauge. We use it because it can test and leave no hole. Thicker testers leave holes.

Our real tester (and the next best thing to taking the cake out and cutting it open) is a narrow-bladed, shiny, stainless steel knife. Just insert the knife into the top of the cake, at the palest part, pull it out, and examine it as you did the wire.

If the knife comes out with batter—back into the oven. If it comes out with a bit of moisture that wipes right off, *don't bake any more, the cake is most likely done*. Moisture condenses on the knife (and wire) even if a cake is overdone.

An additional problem is presented when you are baking fruit in the cake. Apples stay moist, even when the cake is baked. There is no quick solution. Just learn what cooked apple looks like on your knife. And it doesn't look like batter.

Follow Your Nose

Even at the other side of the apartment, we have a way of knowing when a cake is approaching doneness. We follow our nose. You see, when cakes lose a lot of moisture (and are nearly done) they give off a strong aroma, as does anything you bake. If something is beginning to smell done, go take a look. It may be your first clue to get out your cake tester. (It also may be that you've spilled batter on the bottom of the oven—but you'd want to know that anyhow.)

Turning Out

There is nothing more disappointing than baking a cake successfully and then having it break or stick in the turning out.

Remember, these are not breads with sturdy crusts; these are generally quite moist and tender cakes: they don't like handling, and will dent very easily.

So, the first thing to keep in mind is to keep your paws off.

In turning out a cake, barring accidents, you should never handle it at all. Place the business side of a plate over the pan or mold, and, using potholders if it's still hot, turn the whole thing over. If you've greased well, the cake should plop right out (except for *Angel Food* and we'll get to that with the recipe).

If it looks as if you've greased poorly or for some reason some batter has attached itself to the sides of the pan, take a knife and carefully loosen the stuck places.

If it seems that the cake is more firmly entrenched in the pan than it should be and you fear that it is stuck, "tap" it loose. To do this hold the *cooled* pan in one hand and gently rap it with the heel of your free hand, repeatedly, around the outside of the pan. These frequent raps will often loosen even a burnt cake, leaving the scorched part in the pan. Just keep tapping gently but firmly around the outside.

If, after all this, the cake still insists on sticking to the pan, despite greasing, despite loosening with a knife, despite tapping, throw the recipe out, spoon out the cake you've got for a bread pudding, and blame us.

Other Equipment

As for special equipment other than pans and a cake tester, all you need is a wire whisk and a rubber spatula— and if you own a fork and spoon, you can even do without the whisk and spatula.

GINGERBREAD

Preheat oven: 350° to 400°

This is less spicy than some recipes for gingerbread, but it is delightfully moist and light.

1½ cups whole wheat pastry flour	¼ cup unsaturated vegetable oil
1 level teaspoon baking soda	¼ cup maple syrup
½ teaspoon salt	¼ cup honey
½ teaspoon ginger	½ cup yoghurt
1 teaspoon cinnamon	1 large egg

Measure all the dry ingredients into a large bowl and mix well with a fork.

Measure all the wet ingredients into a 2-cup measure and mix well, in the cup.

Add wet ingredients to dry ingredients and mix until uniform.

Pour into a greased, 8-inch-square pan (see "Greasing without Grease" chapter) and bake in preheated oven at 350° to 400° for 30-35 minutes.

Test for doneness (see "Testing" section earlier in this chapter.)

No need to turn out. Cut right in the pan.

PLAIN LEMON CAKE

Preheat oven: 350° to 375°

This is the equivalent of other books' "white cake." But you can't get a white cake from whole wheat flour and honey. It is a plain layer cake, great for icing. (See the chapter on "Icings.")

We only make one layer here, but there is no difficulty in doubling the recipe (or trebling it) so long as you mix in the soda well.

By the way, if you measure your oil in the cup first, all the other measured liquids come out easily.

½ cup unsaturated vegetable oil	½ teaspoon almond extract
⅔ cup honey	2 cups whole wheat pastry flour
½ cup yoghurt	1 teaspoon baking soda
rinds of 2 small lemons	

Measure the oil, honey, and yoghurt into a large bowl and mix well with a whisk.

Grate in the lemon rinds. Add the almond extract.

Measure the flour into a separate bowl, add the soda, and mix well with a fork. Add to the liquid and mix thoroughly.

Pour batter into a greased 9-inch layer-cake pan (see "Greasing without Grease" chapter) and bake in preheated oven at medium-high for about 25 minutes. If the heat of your oven is uneven, and your cake tends to rise more on one side than another, gently rotate the pan in the middle of baking.

Test for doneness (see "Testing" section earlier in this chapter.)

Variation:

If you don't like the lemon tang, you can try substituting 2 teaspoons of vanilla extract for the almond extract and lemon.

APPLE WALNUT LOAF

Here's a simple but great cake. When Floss taught bread baking this was the one cake she included—and the classes always loved it.

Leave the nuts quite coarse; they really make a marvelous contribution that way. And cut the apple into large chunks, too.

In testing, remember, the apple may show on the knife and make the cake look unfinished. The apple will wipe away easily, uncooked batter will not. You'll just have to learn the difference.

½ cup unsaturated vegetable oil	1 teaspoon baking soda
	½ teaspoon salt
1 cup honey	2 cups whole wheat flour
2 large eggs	1 cup walnuts, coarsely chopped
1 teaspoon vanilla	
4 tablespoons yoghurt	1 medium apple, unpeeled

In a large bowl, mix together well the oil, honey, eggs, vanilla, and yoghurt.

Add the soda and salt and mix very well.

Stir in the flour, until thoroughly mixed. Stir in the walnuts.

Wash and core, but do not peel the apple. Cut the apple into largish chunks and add it to the batter.

Pour batter into two 7½-inch loaf pans, well greased (see "Greasing without Grease" chapter). Starting in a cold oven, bake at about 350° for about 50 minutes.

Test for doneness. (See "Testing" section, in this chapter.)

DATE BREAD

The only real work about this handsome and delicious recipe is pitting and cutting the dates. Dates, by the way, are an acid fruit, and neutralize some soda on their own.

1 cup yoghurt	2 cups whole wheat flour
½ cup honey	1 scant teaspoon baking
1 large egg	soda
2 tablespoons *unsaturated*	1 pound moist dates
vegetable oil	

In a large bowl, mix everything, except the dates, together thoroughly.

Pit and quarter the dates and mix them into the batter.

Divide batter between two well-greased 7½-inch loaf pans (see "Greasing without Grease" chapter). Put pans in a cold oven. Turn oven to about 350° and bake for approximately 40 minutes.

Test for doneness. (See "Testing" section, earlier in this chapter.)

DATE-NUT BREAD

1 *recipe* Date Bread	1 *large egg (additional)*
(*above*)	1 *cup broken-up walnuts*

Mix, bake and test as in recipe for *Date Bread* (above).

FRUIT HALF CAKE

This is really just a fruitier variant of the *Date Bread*, and you will have no reason to ask about the silly name once you read the recipe.

1 cup yoghurt
½ cup honey
2 large eggs
2 tablespoons unsaturated vegetable oil
2 cups whole wheat flour
1 scant teaspoon baking soda

½ cup dried apricots
½ cup dates
½ cup raisins
½ cup walnuts, coarsely chopped
½ cup sunflower seeds, shelled

In a large bowl, mix the first six ingredients together.

Cover the apricots with hot water and allow to stand for about 10 minutes. Drain and cut with scissors into quarters or smaller, then add to the batter.

Pit and quarter the dates, and add to the batter.

Add the raisins and walnuts.

Stir in the sunflower seeds until batter is well mixed.

Divide batter between two well-greased 7½-inch loaf pans (see "Greasing without Grease" chapter). Put pans into a cold oven. Bake at about 350° for about 40 minutes. Test for doneness. (See "Testing" section earlier in this chapter.)

Note:

Because of all the fruit, this won't come out as high as the *Date Bread*.

CARROT CAKE

Preheat oven: 350°

This cake is exceptionally moist, a real winner. Don't think of it as a cake with a vegetable in it—think of it as a step on the way to *Asparagus Cake*.

2 large eggs
½ cup unsaturated vegetable oil
1 cup honey
½ cup yoghurt

2 cups whole wheat pastry flour
1 level teaspoon soda
¼ teaspoon salt
1½ teaspoons cinnamon
1 cup carrots, grated

Break the eggs into a large mixing bowl and whisk them until scrambled.

Add the oil, honey and yoghurt, and mix well.

Add the flour, and stir in thoroughly.

Add the soda, salt, cinnamon, and mix very well.

Add grated carrots. Mix in well.

Scrape batter into a greased 9-inch ring mold (see "Greasing without Grease" chapter), and in a preheated oven, bake at about 350° for about 45 minutes.

Test for doneness. (See "Testing" section in this chapter.)

ASPARAGUS CAKE

We can hear the incredulous cries now, echoing *"Asparagus cake?"* Yes, friends, asparagus in a cake, and as delicious a cake as you might want. Asparagus is a very sweet vegetable—especially young and fresh asparagus. Only buy it fresh, while the stems are quite firm and the heads don't yet show signs of flowers—asparagus goes starchy and strong-flavored when it's old.

2 cups whole wheat pastry flour	2 large eggs
½ teaspoon salt	¼ cup nutmeats, chopped medium-coarse
1½ teaspoons baking soda	1½ cups raw asparagus bits, stems and tips both, cut into ½-inch chunks
½ cup unsaturated vegetable oil	
¾ cup honey	
½ cup yoghurt	

Measure the flour, salt and soda into a large bowl and mix together very well.

Add the oil, honey and yoghurt, and mix well.

Break in eggs and stir in thoroughly.

Add the nutmeats and the asparagus.

Scrape into two greased 7-inch loaf pans (see "Greasing

without Grease" chapter). Put pans in a cold oven. Turn oven to about 350° and bake for about 40 to 45 minutes.

Test (see "Testing" section in this chapter), turn out, and enjoy—we know you will.

HONEY CAKE

In the disc jockey's vernacular, honey cake is a "golden oldie."

Honey cake is traditional at certain times of the year, though you can get honey cakes made in Europe (with honey and sugar) all year round. But it's hard to tell how fresh a cake is in the store. You see, honey is a good preservative (as more and more commercial bakers are learning), so a cake rich in honey seems to be fresh for quite a while.

But it is so simple to bake your own, though you do have to watch out for a tendency for the edges to scorch.

⅓	cup unsaturated vegetable oil	1¾	cups whole wheat pastry flour
⅞	cup honey	1	teaspoon baking soda
½	cup yoghurt	½	teaspoon salt
2	large eggs	½	teaspoon ginger
½	teaspoon vanilla extract	½	teaspoon cinnamon

In a large mixing bowl, mix all the wet ingredients together well.

In a 2-cup measure, carefully mix together all the dry ingredients.

Add dry ingredients to wet ingredients and mix both together until uniform.

Scrape batter into one greased 12-inch loaf pan (see "Greasing without Grease" chapter). Put pan in a cold oven. Turn oven to about 350° and bake for about 40 minutes, or until the cake tests done. (See "Testing" section in this chapter.)

VANILLA EGG CAKE

Preheat oven: 350°

Here's a cake similar to the French *Genoise*, but with whole wheat flour instead of white. Like *Genoise*, this cake is raised entirely with eggs, but it doesn't rise as high.

In order for the eggs to beat up really high and frothy, it's necessary to warm the bowl and beaters—and it wouldn't harm to warm the eggs, too. Simply stand the eggs in hot tap water for a few minutes, until they lose their chill. The bowl can be placed in or on a saucepan of simmering water and the beaters can be dipped into the same hot water.

We find a stainless steel bowl excellent for this kind of mixing work, but don't heat it hot enough to cook the eggs.

¾ cup honey	1¼ cups whole wheat
6 large eggs	pastry flour
1 teaspoon vanilla extract	½ cup unsaturated vegetable oil

Measure the honey into a large warmed bowl; add the eggs and vanilla.

Beat with an electric mixer, at medium speed, until *very* thick and *very* high—about 10 minutes (perhaps more). If you've never beaten whole eggs this way before, you'll be surprised at how they rise—we were.

When the eggs are high and thick, add the flour, ¼ cup at a time, folding in gently with a rubber spatula.

When all the flour is in, add the oil, and fold in gently, but thoroughly. The oil folds in readily.

Grease two 9-inch cake pans (see "Greasing without Grease" chapter), and then dust with whole wheat pastry flour.

In an oven preheated to 350°, bake for 35 to 45 minutes, or until the cake is a golden brown and the sides begin to pull away from the pan. Test as described in "Testing" section, in this chapter.

Remove cake from the oven and allow to cool.

Rap around the outside of the pans with your hands, before turning out.

Notes: Serve the layers separately, or fill and ice.

For variations add lemon rind, or substitute 1 teaspoon of almond extract or about 2 tablespoons of rum for the vanilla extract.

NECTARINE-COCONUT CAKE

Preheat oven: 325° to 350°

This is a winner. It looks great, it tastes marvelous, and it's unusual enough to elicit comments even from the most blasé cake eater.

Of course, you can use peaches instead of nectarines —or even apples or strawberries. Fresh fruit is better than frozen for this recipe because fresh fruit has a superior texture.

2	large eggs	1	teaspoon soda
½	cup unsaturated vegetable oil	1	cup desiccated coconut shreds
⅔	cup honey	1½	cups nectarine slices
¾	cup yoghurt	3	teaspoons cinnamon
1	teaspoon vanilla extract		(optional)
2	cups whole wheat pastry flour		

Break the eggs into a large mixing bowl and whisk them until scrambled.

Measure in the oil, honey, yoghurt and vanilla extract, and stir well.

Stir in the flour, then add the soda and stir in very well.

Mix in the coconut, until batter is uniform.

Into a greased (see "Greasing without Grease" chapter) 6-cup Turk's head mold (or any 6-cup mold with a center post), spoon a shallow layer of batter. Add a layer of nectarine slices and a sprinkling of cinnamon. Continue to layer as long as the fruit lasts, then scrape in the remaining batter.

Bake at 325° to 350° for 40 to 45 minutes in a preheated oven.

Test for doneness. (See "Testing" section in this chapter.) But watch out for the wet fruit.

Note:

Be sure you refrigerate this cake if it isn't all eaten the first day: we've found the fruit quick to go bad if it is not refrigerated.

ONE-EGG CUPCAKES

Preheat oven: 350°

Any smooth batter, and most batters that have only small pieces of fruit or nuts, can be used for cupcakes. But here's a delicious plain recipe that is very appropriate for a hand-held cake.

The batter rises higher in these smaller sizes than in cake pans or molds.

We like to use muffin papers, instead of a greased cupcake or muffin pan. These cakes are very light, so if they should stick to the pan instead of turning out easily, they can be completely destroyed by your efforts to get them out. The papers make them much easier to handle.

¼ cup unsaturated vegetable oil	1½ cups whole wheat pastry flour
½ teaspoon vanilla extract	1 level teaspoon baking soda
¾ cup honey	
1 large egg	¼ teaspoon salt
½ cup yoghurt	

Mix the oil, vanilla extract, honey, egg and yoghurt together in a large bowl, beating until well mixed.

Add the flour and mix in.

Add the soda and salt and stir in thoroughly.

Put muffin papers into 16 openings (two 8-hole muffin trays), and divide the batter among them.

Bake in preheated oven for about 20 minutes at about 350°, or until the tops are a golden brown.

Test for doneness. (See "Testing" section in this chapter.)

Note:

Serve plain or ice with a *Cooked Honey Icing* from the "Icings" chapter.

CRANBERRY CAKE

Preheat oven: 350°

Here's a cake with a delightfully chewy texture. If you want it lighter—add some yoghurt to the recipe.

1 large egg	1 level teaspoon baking
1 cup honey	soda
2 cups raw cranberries	1 cup sunflower seeds,
2 cups whole wheat	shelled
pastry flour	grated rind of 1 orange
½ teaspoon salt	

Break egg into your blender container. Add the honey and cranberries and blend at low speed, briefly, until the berries are in chunks. Scrape into a large mixing bowl.

Add the flour and stir in.

Add the salt and soda and mix very well.

Add the sunflower seeds and orange gratings, and stir until very well mixed.

Grease two 6- or 7-inch ring molds (see "Greasing without Grease" chapter) and divide the batter between them.

In a preheated oven, bake at about 350° for 35 to 45 minutes.

Test for doneness. (See "Testing" section early in this chapter.)

Note:

We want to warn you that one of our friends said that this cake could use a bit more honey.

SUNFLOWER CAKE

You do need flour to make a cake, but it needn't be grain flour. Here we grind sunflower seeds down to a flour. So here it is, a wheatless, ryeless, oatless, grainless, "oilless," moist, and rather small cake.

1½ cups sunflower seeds, shelled	½ teaspoon baking soda
	½ cup yoghurt
1 cup desiccated coconut shreds	½ cup honey
	1 large egg

In a blender, grind the sunflower seeds to a flour. Scrape into a large mixing bowl.

Add the coconut shreds and the soda, and mix very well.

In a large measuring cup, mix together the yoghurt, honey and egg. Add to the dry ingredients, and mix until quite uniform.

Grease two 6-inch shaped pans with center posts (see "Greasing without Grease" chapter) and then dust with a bit of whole wheat pastry flour.

Divide the batter between the pans, and bake at 325° to 350° for 40 to 45 minutes.

Test for doneness. (See "Testing" section, earlier in this chapter.)

NO-EGG NO-OIL NUT CAKE

Preheat oven: 300°

Cakes made with nut flour have an extra-special texture, because in home grinding there are always some bits left unground. These bits are delightful surprises to the tongue and teeth when you come across them.

In grinding nuts, be careful that you grind them for as

short a time as you can, and still come up with a flour.
Some nuts, such as walnuts, become quite mushy and oily
with extended grinding.

We like to use hazelnuts (filberts) for our cake flours.
The flavor is excellent and the nuts grind well and easily,
without expressing a great deal of oil.

This recipe yields only one small cake, but don't hesitate to double the recipe. However, in that case, use two
pans.

¼ cup honey	1½ cups nut flour
¼ cup yoghurt	½ teaspoon baking
¼ teaspoon salt	soda

In a medium mixing bowl, mix the honey, yoghurt, and
salt together well.

Stir in the nut flour.

Add the soda and mix everything until uniform.

Scrape the batter into a greased 6½-inch Turk's head pan
(see "Greasing without Grease" chapter). Raise the temperature of your preheated oven to about 325°, and bake
for about 25 minutes. Then shut off the heat and leave
the cake in the oven for another 10 minutes. Test for
doneness. (See "Testing" section in this chapter.)

TURK'S HEAD NUT CAKE

Preheat oven: 350° to 400°

You will need a full cup of ground nuts for this recipe:
¾ cup for the batter and ¼ cup to "flour" the greased
pan.

This cake comes out with a terrific texture. It is light
and high, moist as you could want, soft and really delicious. We've used it as a real "company cake."

½	teaspoon salt	2	large eggs
¼	cup unsaturated vegetable oil	¾	cup nutmeats, ground
1	cup honey	1½	cups whole wheat pastry flour
½	cup yoghurt	1½	teaspoons baking soda
1	teaspoon almond extract	¼	cup nutmeats, ground (additional)

Measure the first five ingredients into a large bowl and mix well.

Break in the eggs and whisk until well distributed.

Add the ¾ cup nutmeats and the flour and stir until uniform.

Stir in the soda and mix until very well blended.

Grease a 6-cup Turk's head pan (see "Greasing without Grease" chapter) and flour it with the remaining ¼ cup of ground nutmeats. That is, dump in the nut flour and tilt, allowing the nuts to stick to the greased pan.

Scrape in the batter. Bake in an oven preheated to 350° to 400° for about 35 minutes.

Test for doneness. (See "Testing" section in this chapter.)

Note:

If this cake shows a slight tendency to stick, rap the sides of the pan until it loosens.

ASPARAGUS TORTE

We've said that cakes shouldn't be handled much after they are removed from the oven. Well, that goes triple for tortes. This recipe is raised solely by a few eggs, and will come tumbling down if you stick your fingers into it. So, hands off! And turn the torte out onto that plate gently.

1   cup nutmeats
3   egg yolks (see
    section on "Separating
    Eggs" earlier in this
    chapter)
¼   cup honey

¼   teaspoon salt
1   cup asparagus bits
½   cup whole wheat
    pastry flour
3   egg whites

Grind the nutmeats at slow speed in your blender and reserve them in a large bowl. (Don't clean the blender yet —you aren't finished.)

Into the blender put the egg yolks, honey, salt, and asparagus chunks. Blend at medium speed to a puree. Scrape into a bowl, over the ground nuts, and mix until uniform.

Add the pastry flour and stir very well.

In another large bowl, beat the whites until they are very stiff. Fold in the asparagus mixture.

Grease a 9-inch ring mold (see "Greasing without Grease" chapter) and scrape in the batter gently, being careful to leave as many bubbles intact as you can.

Starting in a cold oven, bake torte for 5 minutes with temperature set at highest heat, then reduce the setting to medium (about 350°), and bake for about 25 minutes more.

DON'T TEST! The top of the batter will *look* done and solid—it won't ripple if you give it a very gentle shake.

NO-GRAIN CAKE

Preheat oven: 350°

There is no simpler cake recipe than this one.

The flavor is excellent and the texture is quite light, but it won't rise high.

2   cups filberts
    (hazelnuts)

2   large eggs
½   cup maple syrup

Grind the nuts into a flour with some bits left in it. Reserve.

Put the eggs and syrup into a large, warmed bowl and beat them at medium-high speed, about 5 to 7 minutes, until the mixture is pale-yellow and quite high.

Reduce the speed and beat in the nut flour.

Grease well an 8½-inch loaf pan (see chapter on "Greasing without Grease").

Bake for 35 to 40 minutes in a preheated oven at about 350°. Test for doneness. (See "Testing" section, earlier in this chapter.)

Allow to cool. Run a knife around the inside of the pan gently. Rap with your hand around the outside of the pan until the cake loosens, then turn it out.

Note:

This cake will not keep all the rise it gets in the baking, but it does keep a nicely domed look.

HOLIDAY FRUITCAKE

Here's a cake that comes out heavy and chewy and fruity. It's just the thing for the holidays, and relatively quick for a fruitcake.

It is expensive to make, but wholesome and filling: a little bit makes for a satisfying dessert, and it keeps well.

4	large eggs	1	cup almond nutmeats, slivered
¾	cup honey		
½	cup unsaturated vegetable oil	1	cup dried figs, scissored small
3	tablespoons orange peel, grated	1	cup pitted dates, quartered
2	cups whole wheat flour	½	cup dried apples, scissored small
½	cup sesame seeds, with hulls	½	cup filberts, coarsely chopped
1½	cups raisins		
½	cup sunflower seeds, shelled	½	cup dried apricots, quartered
1½	cups walnut meats, broken		

Mix the first five ingredients together in a bowl until smooth.

Add the remaining ingredients and mix together well.

Grease your containers well (see "Greasing without Grease" chapter). You can use small ring molds, loaf pans, or muffin cups.

Scrape the mixture into your containers. Leave room for a little rise in the baking.

Bake in a slow (about 300°) oven. Ring molds should bake in about 1 hour and 20 minutes; muffins in about 50 minutes; a 7-inch loaf pan in about 1 hour and 20 minutes.

Test for doneness. (See "Testing" section in this chapter.)

ANGEL FOOD CAKE

Preheat oven: 325°

Be certain that you've mastered the technique of separating eggs (see "Separating Eggs" at the beginning of this chapter) before you tackle *Angel Food Cake*. We've found it desirable, when separating this many eggs, to drain off one white at a time into a small bowl before pouring it into the large bowl for beating. That way, if you *do* spill any yolk in with the white, you've only spoiled one white.

In this recipe we use cream of tartar (tartaric acid) which is a by-product of wine fermentation. It is an "acceptable" chemical, like baking soda, but one which we prefer to use only very occasionally, and in small amounts. In fact, this is the only use we have for cream of tartar, so one small can will last us for years.

We recommend that you beat the eggs by hand, not by machine because we've found that the texture of hand-beaten whites is much better for angel cake. Use a large wire whisk and a large mixing bowl—and don't spill the egg white on your shoes.

A two-piece angel-food pan is needed for this recipe.

The baked cake is just too difficult to remove from a one-piece cake pan. DO NOT GREASE AT ALL. If you do, the cake will collapse in the baking. The eggs must have the ungreased pan walls to climb up and hold on to.

The only way to test this cake in cooking is to look for the golden brown surface, that means it's done.

And what do you mean, "What am I going to do with all those egg yolks?"! Just see our recipe for *Zabaglione* in the "Custards" chapter (page 104).

whites of 12 large eggs *(1½ cups)*	*1* *teaspoon almond extract*
½ *teaspoon salt*	*1½ cups Maple Sugar*
1¼ *teaspoons cream of* *tartar*	*(see page 212)*
1 *tablespoon vanilla* *extract*	*1* *scant cup whole wheat* *pastry flour*

In a large mixing bowl, beat the egg whites with a wire whisk until frothy.

Sprinkle the salt and cream of tartar over the surface, and continue to beat until the beaten whites hold a small peak well (about 5 minutes).

Measure in the extracts and beat in well.

Sprinkle in gradually only 1 cup of the maple sugar and beat for another minute, until very well mixed.

In a large measuring cup or small bowl, mix together the remaining ½ cup of sugar and the pastry flour. Toss gently with a fork until any clumps are broken.

A quarter or a third of a cup at a time, sprinkle this flour-and-sugar mixture over the surface of the beaten egg whites. With a rubber spatula, fold the mixture in gently but thoroughly. You want to mix the flour in well, but you don't want to break down too many of the bubbles you've beaten in.

Gently scrape the batter into an *ungreased* 10-inch angel-food pan and place in the middle of your preheated oven.

Bake at medium-low (325 to 350°) for 65 to 70 minutes, until the top is a golden brown and shows no moisture.

When cake is done, remove from the oven and turn upside down until completely cool. The cake will not fall out of the ungreased pan; this upside-down position helps prevent sagging as the cake cools.

When cake is cool, run a knife around the inside of the pan. Press on the bottom of the pan to remove your cake. To remove the rest of the pan, run a knife around the bottom of the cake and outside the center post. Or you can serve the cake right on this inner part of the pan as we like to do.

The cake keeps very well.

Yield: one 10-inch cake

Option:

Angel food cake can be made without any cream of tartar, but it will not come out quite as high. Your cake will have a slight tendency to sag and the bubbles will be a little larger, but the texture and flavor are still great.

11

Icings and Cake Fillings

Icings are traditionally made with confectioners' sugar—a combination of white sugar (ground superfine) and cornstarch. It dissolves without a trace, giving you a very smooth icing.

As they are, maple syrup and honey are generally too liquid for icings. After all, the icing has to stay where you put it. Well, we are very pleased to announce (a little fanfare, maestro, please) that you can have icings made with honey or maple syrup which are very close to sugar icings, and usually tastier.

Maple Sugar Icings

First of all, look at our recipe for *Maple Sugar* (see "Miscellany" chapter). It is not hard to make, and gives you a dry sugar which can be ground rather fine (though not as fine as confectioners' sugar), and yet is still full of the minerals that make maple syrup so desirable.

We give only four recipes using *Maple Sugar* for icing, but once you've tried them, you'll want to go over all your old icing recipes, and remake them with this delicious and healthy alternative.

Maple Sugar can't be ground as fine as white, so the icing texture is a little "gritty"—but who cares?

MAPLE-LEMON ICING

The lemon tang overpowers the maple flavor in this sweet and lemon-rich icing.

1 cup Maple Sugar *(see "Miscellany" chapter)*
grated peel (yellow only) of 1 medium lemon

¼ cup instant milk powder
2 tablespoons water (approximately)

Put the *Maple Sugar*, grated lemon peel, and milk powder into a small mixing bowl.

Add 1 tablespoon water and mix well with a fork. Add as much of the second tablespoon as you need to make a thick paste—but not too thick, you want to be able to spread it. If you've used too much water, allow the icing to sit in the bowl to thicken somewhat before spreading.

With a butter knife, spread thinly and gently over the surface and sides of your cake.

Yield: enough to ice one single-layer 8-inch cake

Note:

Left overnight, this icing will dry almost hard.

You can substitute whole milk for the water, but do use some instant powdered milk, too, or you won't get the texture right.

MAPLE-ORANGE ICING

Even if you're able to get organic oranges, and they are available pretty much year-round, scrub the skin anyway.

1 cup Maple Sugar *(see "Miscellany" chapter)*
grated peel (orange only) of ½ large orange

¼ cup instant milk powder
2 tablespoons fresh orange juice (approximately)

Prepare as *Maple-Lemon Icing* (see above).

Yield: enough to ice one single-layer 8-inch cake

MAPLE-BUTTER ICING (Vanilla)

A little butter makes for a very smooth icing, and one that doesn't dry out. But it is more work. The butter must be "creamed," that is, worked with a fork until it is broken down and spread around, so that the sugar may be worked into it. But it does make for a grand texture. Do not use salted butter, no matter how "lightly salted."

2 tablespoons sweet butter
1 cup Maple Sugar (see "Miscellany" chapter)

1 teaspoon vanilla extract (or more, to taste)
2 tablespoons water (approximately)

Cream the butter with a fork.

Blend in the *Maple Sugar*.

Blend in the vanilla and taste.

Add enough water to make into a thick but spreadable paste.

Spread with a knife, gently, over the surface and sides of your cake.

Yield: enough for a single-layer 8-inch cake

SHERRY-MAPLE ICING

A wine icing makes a marvelous topping for a plain cake. We use a New York State cream sherry, but any sweet dessert wine will probably do.

2 tablespoons sweet butter
1 cup Maple Sugar (see "Miscellany" chapter)

½ teaspoon vanilla extract
2 tablespoons cream sherry (approximately)

Make up as *Maple-Butter Icing* (see above), using as much of the wine as necessary to make a thick but spreadable paste.

Yield: enough for a single-layer 8-inch cake

Honey Icings

Yes, honey *is* usually too thin to use in an icing, and you can't cook it down and get honey sugar as we got *Maple Sugar*, but, with a little imagination, there are ways around the problem.

In the following recipes we will thicken the honey, either by cooking it, or by the addition of thickeners. Read on. We think you'll be surprised.

HONEY-BUTTER ICING

For this tasty icing, there is no spreading, you just pour or spoon it on. The cooking thickens the honey enough for it to stay where you put it, and then it half-hardens to something like a candy. The butter gives it a butterscotch-like flavor.

⅓ *cup honey*   2 *tablespoons sweet butter*

In a small saucepan, bring ingredients to a simmer over low heat and continue to simmer for 10 minutes more or until the color just begins to darken.

Remove from the heat and allow the bubbles to die down, then spoon over cupcakes or pour over a cake.

Yield: enough for a batch of *Cupcakes* or for an 8-inch layer. (See "Cakes.")

Uncooked Honey Icings

The following half dozen recipes are made primarily in the blender, all with pretty much the same technique:

Measure your honey into the blender;

Add a flavoring or fruit (if any) and blend in well;

Add instant dry milk powder for a thickener, and blend in well;

Scrape into a bowl and allow to stand a bit to thicken —the milk powder absorbs liquid;

Then spread on as an icing or filling.

These tend to be rather sweet, but they are fine as icings for unsweet cakes.

PLAIN HONEY ICING

In this basic recipe, we use no flavoring other than the honey itself, cutting the sweetness somewhat with the milk. If you wish to add flavorings, try a teaspoon of vanilla or almond extract, or a teaspoon of finely-ground star anise.

½ cup honey   1   cup instant milk powder

Measure the honey into the blender and turn it on, set for medium speed.

If you are using a flavoring, add it now.

Add the milk powder a bit at a time, until quite thick.

Allow to stand for a half hour before using.

Yield: a bit more than ½ cup of icing

CHESTNUT ICING

Here's a most unusual recipe, for an icing or a filling. See page 210 for how to cook chestnuts.

½ cup honey   ½ cup instant milk
½ cup cooked chestnut   powder
  pulp, packed

Measure the honey into your blender.

Add the chestnuts, and pushing nuts toward blades with a rubber spatula, chop to a purée. REMEMBER, SHUT THE MOTOR OFF BEFORE YOU PUT THE SPATULA IN.

Add the milk powder and blend until very smooth—helping with the spatula as needed.

Allow to stand about ½ hour before using.

Yield: about 1 cup

LEMON MILK ICING

Lemon is perfect in icing—especially the peel, which gives us lemon flavor without lemon sourness.

½ cup honey   ¾ cup instant milk
grated peel (yellow only)   powder
  of 1 medium lemon

Measure the honey and the grated lemon peel into your blender and blend for a moment.

Add the milk powder and blend for a minute, or until very smooth.

Allow to stand for ½ hour before using.

Yield: a bit more than ½ cup

COFFEE ICING

Feel free to use a coffee substitute instead of the decaffeinated. The tablespoon is enough for 3 strong cups of coffee, so use a corresponding amount of the substitute.

The full cup of honey makes this recipe harder to blend. If you have difficulty, SHUT OFF THE BLENDER, stir with a rubber spatula, then turn the blender on again.

1 cup honey   1 cup instant milk
1 level tablespoon instant   powder
  decaffeinated coffee

Measure the honey and coffee into the blender container and process briefly until well mixed.

Add the milk powder, and blend for a minute or two, until smooth and even.

Yield: about 1¼ cups or enough to ice and fill a 2-layer 9-inch cake

APRICOT ICING

This is tops—the tastiest icing you can imagine. The tart dried apricots and the sweet honey are a dynamite combination. And, it's chock full of vitamin A, minerals, calcium, and it even has some protein.

Apricots, even soaked, are difficult to process. SHUT OFF YOUR BLENDER and help the mixture along with a rubber spatula, as often as needed to get everything chopped. But don't strive for absolute smoothness. You can't get it. The mixture will be mottled brown and tan, and somewhat lumpy. Not to worry.

1 cup dried apricots	½ cup instant milk
1 cup honey	powder

Set the apricots in a bowl of very hot tap water for 10 minutes, then drain well.

Meanwhile, measure the honey into your blender container.

Add the drained apricots, and blend until well chopped.

Blend in the milk powder. (This will be a very thick mixture.) Use immediately, or it will get too thick to spread.

Yield: enough for a 2-layer, 9-inch cake

Confession time:

We made a batch of this for testing, and didn't use it for icing but left it around in a bowl. After a few days, the apricots had absorbed so much liquid that the "icing" was too thick to spread. What did we do? Not throw it out, you can bet. We ate it as a "spoon candy," scooping up little teaspoonfuls and licking it off. Not to be believed.

COCONUT ICING

A cup of dried coconut shreds is enough to make the honey quite thick. In order to get the milk powder in, we'll heat the blended honey and coconut in a saucepan, to soften and thin the honey, and *then* mix in the powdered milk. You're not really cooking anything, just warming it enough to thin it out.

The milk powder is needed—without it, the icing would be thick enough but unbearably sweet.

1 cup honey	1 cup instant milk
1 cup desiccated coconut	powder
shreds	

In the blender, process the honey and coconut together until well mixed. Don't try to make it really smooth.

Scrape into a 1-quart saucepan, and put over a low heat, until the mixture is a bit more liquid.

Remove from the heat and mix in the milk powder well.

Yield: enough for topping and filling a 2-layer, 9-inch cake

ORANGE DRIZZLE

What is a drizzle? Well, it is a sort of soft icing. It is an icing without body but with lots of flavor. Instead of sitting on top of your cake, it soaks right in, which means that you should eat a drizzled-on cake as soon as you drizzle it or you run the risk of sogginess.

1 juicy orange	1 to 2 tablespoons honey

Wash, peel, and pit the orange, then liquefy it in the blender.

Add 1 to 2 tablespoons of honey to taste, and blend in.

Pour onto your cake.

Yield: enough for one 9-inch cake ring

Fillings

While many of the preceding icings can be used as fillings, here follow two fillings that won't serve as icings —unless you're desperate.

CLOVE CAKE FILLING

This is a filling that has a texture much like a pudding.

½ cup honey
¼ cup water
¼ teaspoon ground cloves

1 rounded tablespoon arrowroot starch

Mix all the ingredients together in a 1-quart saucepan.

Cook over medium heat, stirring constantly, for about 4 minutes, or until rather thick.

Cool, and spread over the bottom layer of a cake.

Yield: enough to fill one 8- or 9-inch layer cake

Note:

This particular recipe can be varied enormously. Use any fruit juice, ground spice or extract—anything you can think of—keeping the same proportions.

BANANA FILLING

This is almost a jam. Use only the very ripest of bananas.

1 pound of bananas (weighed with skins on)

½ cup honey

Peel the bananas and mash them in a 2-quart pot.

Add the honey, stir well, and cook over very low heat until thick: about 40 minutes.

Remove from the heat and cool.

Yield: enough to fill one 9-inch layer cake

12

Cookies

Did you steal cookies from the cookie jar when you were a child? What kid doesn't? Well, cookies, like so many other goodies, *are* largely carbohydrate—made from flour and sugars—and while carbohydrates have a place in the diet (your liver can't function properly without them), they shouldn't predominate at the expense of protein and other food elements.

Which is our way of saying that if people, kids *and* adults, are going to eat cookies anyway, why not make these goodies as healthy as possible? And why not make rather small batches of them so that your family (or yourself) can't indulge in cookie orgies?

You can let your kids or your spouse or yourself eat these cookies (in moderate amounts) without feeling that you are compromising their health or your own: most of them contain extra protein bonuses like eggs and milk powder. Some of the recipes call for no flour at all. And, best of all, these cookies taste delicious!

Once you understand the principles, cookie recipes are among the easiest to invent or adapt. This chapter contains basic recipes which you can vary to make your own cookie favorites.

LACY OATMEAL COOKIES

This is like putting your best foot forward. This excellent cookie has a chewy texture and rich flavor. And the holes that form in the baking fascinate young and old alike.

2 large eggs	1 teaspoon almond extract
½ cup unsaturated vegetable oil	1 cup instant milk powder
¾ cup honey	2 cups rolled oats

Break the eggs into a large mixing bowl and whisk until scrambled.

Measure the oil and honey into the same cup. Add to eggs and stir.

Add the almond extract and milk powder and stir.

Add the rolled oats and mix very well.

Spoon mixture onto 2 greased baking sheets (see "Greasing without Grease" chapter), leaving room for quite a bit of spread.

Do not preheat oven. Starting cool, bake in a medium-low (about 325°) oven for about 20 to 25 minutes, until the cookies get thin and bubbly. Don't allow these to really brown: the flavor decreases as the browning increases.

Remove trays from the oven and lift the cookies off the sheets with a pancake turner. Place cookies on dishes to cool. The cookies will still be soft at this stage: they harden and set as they cool.

If your cookies have spread so much that they join, cut them apart.

Yield: about 20 large, thin cookies

OATMEAL-COCONUT COOKIES

The coconut shreds give these cookies extra eye appeal.

Unlike the cookies in the previous recipe, these will stay thick.

2 large eggs	1 cup instant milk powder
¼ cup unsaturated vegetable oil	1 cup desiccated coconut shreds
½ cup honey	2 cups rolled oats
1 teaspoon almond extract	

Break the eggs into a large mixing bowl and whisk them until well scrambled.

Add the oil, honey and almond extract. Mix well.

Add the milk powder. Mix well.

Mix the coconut in well, until all of it is wet.

Add the oats and mix everything until rather uniform in appearance.

Grease 2 large baking sheets (see "Greasing without Grease" chapter). Drop the batter onto the sheets by the tablespoonful, leaving a little room for spreading.

Starting in a warm oven, bake cookies about 20 minutes at medium-low temperature (about 325°). Be careful. The bottoms of these scorch easily.

Yield: about 20 cookies

NUTS AND WHEAT COOKIES

Nuts in combination with whole wheat flour result in a very rich flavor. Filberts are called for, but Brazil nuts will do, too.

1 cup filberts (hazelnuts)	½ cup honey
1 cup whole wheat pastry flour	¼ cup unsaturated vegetable oil

In your blender or with a grater, grind the nuts to a flour, then dump them into a large mixing bowl.

Add the remaining ingredients and mix well.

Knead gently, working the dough into a cohesive ball. (This is not like kneading bread: knead only to get everything to stick together so you can cut it easily.)

Form into a sausage shape, about 2 inches in diameter and 7 or 8 inches long. (This "sausage" can be stored in your refrigerator for a day or so, if you don't have time to bake it now.)

Cut dough into ½-inch slices. Then cut each slice in half. Flatten each piece to a ¼-inch thickness and set on a large, greased baking sheet (see "Greasing without Grease" chapter). These cookies will not spread, so there's no need to leave room between them.

Do not preheat oven. Starting in a cold oven, bake at medium temperature (about 350°) for 20 to 25 minutes, or until the bottoms begin to brown. Don't allow the bottoms of these cookies to scorch.

Eat cookies as they are or ice with *Boiled Honey Icing* (see page 172).

Yield: about 30 cookies

ORANGE-COCONUT COOKIES

Preheat oven: 350° (medium)

This recipe is only mildly sweet. If you like very sweet stuff, add another tablespoon or two of honey.

1 large egg	3 tablespoons fresh orange
¼ cup unsaturated	juice (from same orange)
vegetable oil	1 cup whole wheat flour
½ cup honey	1 cup desiccated coconut —
grated peel (orange only) of	shreds
1 medium-sized orange	

Break the egg into a large mixing bowl and beat lightly.

Add the oil and honey.

Grate the outer peel of the orange into the bowl.

Add the orange juice and mix everything together well.

Mix the flour and coconut in very well.

Spoon the batter by tablespoonfuls onto a greased baking sheet (see "Greasing without Grease" chapter).

Bake at medium for about 15 minutes, or until the tops begin to brown.   Yield: about 20 cookies

MAPLE-PECAN COOKIES

Even unshelled pecans can be very expensive. Also, it can be difficult to open them and still keep the nuts intact. If you can't get the pecan halves out without breaking them, don't raise a sweat over it. The halves are just decoration: add those broken nuts to the batter.

1   large egg
¼   cup unsaturated
     vegetable oil
¾   cup maple syrup
1   cup whole wheat flour
1   cup instant milk powder
rind of ½ a lemon, freshly
     grated

3   tablespoons fresh lemon
     juice (from the same
     lemon)
1   cup coarsely chopped
     (or just broken up)
     pecans
26 pecan halves (for
     topping)

Break the egg into a large mixing bowl and beat lightly.

Mix in the oil and syrup.

Add the flour and milk powder and mix very well.

Add the lemon rind and juice, then the chopped pecans.

Mix well until the batter is fairly even.

Spoon the batter by tablespoonfuls onto 1 or 2 greased baking sheets (see "Greasing without Grease" chapter). These cookies will spread slightly, so give them room.

Top each with a ½ pecan.

Starting in a warm oven, bake at medium (about 350°) for 20 to 25 minutes.

Yield: about 26 cookies

MAPLE-PECAN ALL-NUTS

Nut-flour cookies don't bake as hard as do most wheat-flour cookies: they stay chewy. But the oils in the nuts don't keep as well as the oils in baked wheat, so don't expect to store these cookies. However, for the week or so these stay fresh, they are delicious, with a very special flavor.

2 cups mixed filberts and walnuts shelled (or other nuts)	1 large egg ¾ cup maple syrup ½ cup pecan pieces

Grind the 2 cups of nuts into a flour. Pour into a large mixing bowl.

Add the egg, syrup and ½ cup of pecans. Mix well.

Spoon the batter by teaspoonfuls onto a greased baking sheet (see "Greasing without Grease" chapter).

Starting in a cold oven, bake at medium-low (about 325°) for about 45 minutes, or until firm.

Yield: about 18 cookies

ALL-NUT COOKIES

There are some people who don't like the very definite flavor of filberts (hazelnuts). However, put them into a recipe like this and the strong taste is an asset. If you get tired of shelling the filberts, substitute some walnuts. In fact, include ¼ to ½ cup of walnuts whenever you try this recipe.

2 cups mixed filbert⠀⠀⠀⠀⅜ cup honey
⠀⠀and walnut nutmeats⠀⠀½ cup additional nutmeats
2 large eggs

Grind the 2 cups of nutmeats to a fine flour. Pour into a large mixing bowl.

Mix in the eggs and honey.

Chop the remaining ½ cup of nutmeats coarsely. Add to the batter and mix well.

Spoon by tablespoonfuls onto a greased baking sheet (see "Greasing without Grease" chapter). You can expect these cookies to spread some in the baking.

Starting in a cold oven, bake at medium-low (about 325°) for about 45 minutes, or until rather firm on top and browning on the bottom.

Yield: 12 large cookies

SEED COOKIES

Seeds are exceptionally healthful foods: this part of the plant—still alive, even though it may seem dry and dead—contains many valuable nutrients packed into little space.

1 cup unhulled sesame⠀⠀⠀½ cup honey
⠀⠀seeds⠀⠀⠀⠀⠀⠀⠀⠀⠀⠀⠀1 large egg
1 cup desiccated coconut
⠀⠀shreds

Grind the sesame seeds to a flour. Pour into a large mixing bowl.

Add the remaining ingredients and mix very well.

Spoon onto a greased baking sheet (see "Greasing without Grease" chapter).

Starting in a cold oven, bake for about 30 minutes at low temperature (about 300°). Yield: about 16 cookies

NO-GRAIN COCONUTS

It is hard to imagine a cookie recipe that could be simpler, faster, or more delicious than this one. Even a confirmed coconut disliker (Floss's mother) liked them.

2 large eggs	2 cups desiccated coconut
½ cup honey	shreds

Mix the eggs and honey together in a large mixing bowl until very well blended.

Add the coconut shreds and stir very well—you want the honey well distributed.

Spoon the batter by teaspoonfuls onto a greased baking sheet (see "Greasing without Grease" chapter).

Starting in a cold oven bake at medium temperature (about 350°) until the cookie bottoms brown (about 10 to 12 minutes). Then turn carefully, with a pancake turner, and bake on the other side for about 5 minutes.

The bottoms of the cookies would scorch before the tops got baked if you didn't turn them.

Yield: about 20 to 24 shiny cookies

13

Snacks

Snacks can be good foods, relaxing foods. They give your hands and your mouth something to do while your mind is elsewhere. You read a book, your hands open peanut shells, you jaw chomps—very relaxing.

But there are some snacks that don't paint so attractive a picture. For example, some snacks are so heavily salted that they constitute a menace to anyone with circulation problems.

Now, there is no point in your saying you don't eat a lot of salt or salty stuff. Do you eat canned foods? Heavily salted, many of them. Cold cuts? Forget it. Even sweets like cake mixes have salt in them. Now, that's not quite so relaxing.

The snack food industry is a huge industry, with huge profits, and a great deal to answer for if they could be brought to account: they probably peddle more junk and unhealth than any other part of America's food business.

Flavorings, colorings, preservatives—have you ever read the labels on any of the commercial snacks? Incredible! So much of this stuff reads as if it should be made in a test tube and not a kitchen.

Well, you needn't participate in the ripoff—you can make your own.

Naturalest Snacks

There are certain snacks we don't include in this book

because they don't require preparation—raisins, and other dried fruits, nuts and seeds of all kinds, fresh fruits. These are the preferred snacks, the ones we eat most often, the ones any adult should choose.

For kids, the problem can be different: they are so much influenced by what they see on TV and what they see their friends eating, that they will often demand an unhealthy product in preference to a natural and healthy snack.

You can belt the kid and let it go at that, or you can try to substitute something healthy for the unhealthy— something that may even look like the unhealthy product.

Substitutes

Our recipes for *Popcorn Balls* and *Popcorn Snack* are good examples of healthy substituting. You see, the only thing that makes popcorn an *un*good goody is what is usually added to the snack—lots of butter and salt, saturated oils, preservatives, colorings, and so forth, all of which can be found in a bag of prepopped popcorn. By itself, popcorn is an excellent treat, basically low in calories and fairly high in protein.

Snacks like *Soy Crunch* (any of the Bean Crunches) can be tucked into a lunch box. They'll masquerade as salted nuts. They don't have the dangers of the salted nuts, but they do have a good deal of valuable protein.

Bean Crunch

We don't list every bean in the world, but you could make this snack with almost every one of them.

Think of them as substitutes for salted nuts. Remember, the oil in nuts is not of the stablest, and it may go rancid by the time you buy the nuts. Salt hides the rancid taste of oil, which means you could be eating rancid oil and never know it.

Then there is the salt itself. Salt is very bad for your

circulation. Next to sugar, it's the biggest no-no in the great American diet.

Soybeans are naturally high in potassium, which tends to counteract and balance the effects of salt in your system. While sodium is easily available, potassium is not, and so you have to look around for foods which are rich in potassium.

All these Bean Crunches are fun treats, different, easy to make, inexpensive, and quite low-calorie, too.

Aside from cooking the beans themselves, we use no salt in these recipes, but we do use many other flavorings. The chick peas can be cooled and eaten right from the pot, but the soybeans are just a bit bland on their own.

BASIC SOY CRUNCH

Let's start from scratch. You'll need a large pot for boiling the beans, and three large baking sheets for making the Crunch.

1 pound dry soybeans   *1 tablespoon salt*
6 cups hot water

Put the beans in a large pot, wash them by covering them with water and then pouring it off.

Cover the beans with 6 cups of hot water and the salt and leave them, covered, to stand overnight. (Don't let the beans stand any longer or they will begin to ferment. Even overnight you may get some froth on the surface of the water—not to worry.)

The next morning, boil the beans in the same water until they are crisp-done, about ¾ hour. You don't want them soft. You should now have about 6 cups of cooked beans.

With a strainer, scoop out about 2 cups of the cooked beans, and allow them to drain well.

Sprinkle the beans onto an ungreased baking sheet. Spread them out so that they are in a single layer. (If you wish to treat the rest of the beans the same way, go ahead and do that now. If you wish to add a flavoring, read the next recipe.)

To cook, place the tray in the middle of your oven and roast at about 300° until brown and crunchy—about 50 minutes.

Yield: about 1½ cups of Crunch

Note:

The variations on these beans are limited only by the variety of powdered flavorings on your herb shelf.

You can use any powdered herb or flavoring you like: 1½ teaspoons of powdered onion, for instance; ¼ teaspoon powdered sage; etc.

But if your mind's eye turns to things like seasoned salt, barbeque flavoring, hickory salt, and the like, be certain you read the labels. Many of these products contain chemical flavorings, anticoagulants, and MSG.

GARLIC-KELP CRUNCH

To make flavored Crunches, you need a 2-quart covered container of some kind. Perhaps a reusable ½-gallon ice cream box—left over from the days when you bought ice cream rather than made your own.

| 2 | cups cooked soybeans (see above) | 1 | teaspoon powdered garlic |
| | | ¼ | teaspoon granulated kelp |

Allow 2 cups of crisp-cooked soybeans to drain well, and then put them into a covered 2-quart container.

Add the flavorings to the container.

Cover and shake very well, until all the beans are coated with some of the flavoring.

Pour soybeans over a large, ungreased baking sheet, and spread around until you have a single layer.

Roast in a low oven (about 300°) for about 50 minutes, until brown and crunchy.

Yield: about 1½ cups

OILED CRUNCH

We've never seen a commercial variety of Crunch without oil. Oil gives it more snap, but it also adds problems: the Crunch must be refrigerated (or the oil may go rancid) and the calories increase. The 1 teaspoon of oil that we use doesn't add many calories.

2 cups cooked soybeans (see   1 teaspoon unsaturated
   Basic Soy Crunch, above)   vegetable oil

Drain 2 cups of cooked soybeans and put them into a 2-quart container with a cover.

Add the oil, cover, shake well, and cook as described in Basic Soy Crunch (see above).

CHICK PEAS

Chick peas (garbanzos) are an excellent source of many minerals, of vitamins, and of good vegetable protein. They don't need much done with them to make them an attractive snack. Just cooked, they are tasty. We like to eat them by the handful, or toss them into a salad.

Don't overcook chick peas. Mushy beans make an unattractive snack.

1 cup dry chick peas   1 teaspoon salt
4 cups water

Soak the beans in the water and salt for about 4 hours, and then cook for about 15 minutes.

Drain off the water and cool the chick peas.

Yield: more than 2 cups

CHICK CRUNCH

To turn garbanzos into a Crunch, boil them only 10 minutes in the original cooking.

2 cups crisp-cooked chick peas (see Chick Peas, *above)*

Drain the chick peas and spread them over an ungreased baking sheet in a single layer.

Bake in a medium oven (about 350°) for about 35 minutes, or until browned and crisp enough to rattle.

Yield: about 1½ cups of Crunch

KELP-CHICK CRUNCH

We like to use granulated kelp wherever we can— especially nowadays with fish getting more and more expensive and becoming a smaller part of our diet. Kelp supplies iodine that is so important to the functioning of the thyroid gland.

*2 cups crisp-cooked chick   ½ teaspoon granulated
    peas (see above,* Chick   kelp
    Peas)   dash salt (optional)*

Drain the beans and spoon them into a 2-quart covered container.

Add the kelp, and salt if desired.

Shake very well, until well mixed, then pour in a single layer on an ungreased baking sheet.

Bake in a medium oven (about 350°) for about 35 minutes.

Yield: about 1½ cups

Variations:

For other variations, see the suggestions at the end of *Basic Soy Crunch, above.*

BLACK-EYED PEAS

When properly cooked as a vegetable, these beans get a mushy texture which is appropriate to their flavor. For the kind of Bean Crunch we're making here, however, the beans must be fairly firm when they go into the oven, or they will all but disappear in the baking. We have a simple solution: *we don't precook the black-eyed peas at all.*

1 cup dry black-eyed peas   1 teaspoon salt
4 cups hot water

Pour the beans, water, and salt into a pot, and allow to soak for 4 hours. DO NOT PRECOOK.

BLACK-EYED KELP CRUNCH

We don't eat these soaked beans raw, they have too green a flavor for our taste, but they make a very crunchy Crunch.

2 cups soaked black-eyed peas   1 teaspoon granulated kelp salt, to taste

Shake, spread, and bake as in *Kelp-Chick Crunch* (see above).

BLACK-EYED GARLIC CRUNCH

2 cups soaked black-eyed peas   ½ teaspoon powdered garlic, to taste
    ½ teaspoon salt, to taste

Mix, spread and bake as in *Kelp-Chick Crunch* (see above).

SALT-FREE POPCORN

Don't butter it, don't salt it heavily, don't spice it, don't cook it in heavy oils, and popcorn is a nutritious and delightful snack. It has gotten a bad reputation because of what is done with it, not because of what it is itself.

But the same is true of popcorn as of anything cooked with oil; oil can go rancid if left around. So plan to eat your popcorn soon after popping.

We'll give specific proportions for a 3-quart pot below, but, as a rule of thumb, you can lightly oil and cover the bottom of any standard-shape covered pot with a single layer of popcorn kernels, and that will about fill the pot with popped corn.

1 to 2 tablespoons   *½ cup popping corn*
unsaturated vegetable oil

Oil the bottom of the pot with a thin layer of a light oil. Pour in the popping corn and shake the pot to oil the kernels. Cover pot tightly.

Turn the heat to high and begin to shake the pot. Keep shaking while the corn is heating and for the first few seconds of popping.

As the popping sounds come closer together, stop shaking. Leave the heat on until the last lone pop dies away.

Turn the heat off and allow pan to stand for a moment (to allow any last strays to pop off). Eat hot.

Yield: about 3 quarts

Note:

With a bit more than 1 tablespoon of oil for popping, this popcorn has less than 150 calories per *quart*, and virtually no sodium.

Variations:

If you're not used to unsalted stuff, add 1 tablespoon of kelp to the hot popcorn, then salt to taste and mix well.

For *Cheese Popcorn*, add 3 tablespoons of grated Parmesan cheese to hot popcorn and stir *very* well.

POPCORN BALLS

These are great fun, both to make and to eat. But don't handle the balls until the honey has cooled enough to be safe. On the other hand, if you wait too long, the honey may become too hard to roll into balls.

1 popped recipe Salt-Free Popcorn *(see above)*	*½ cup honey*

Pour the popped popcorn into a large bowl.

Put the honey into a small saucepan, bring to a boil over low heat, and simmer for 10 minutes.

Pour the honey over the popcorn and, with a pair of forks, begin to toss the corn gently, to get as much of it covered with honey as you can.

When just cool enough to handle, press large handfuls together into balls (you decide on the size you prefer). Don't be too gentle or the balls won't stick. Don't be too rough or you'll crumble the popcorn.

As the balls are formed, place them on a clean dish. Wrap each ball in waxed paper. These will keep for a week or so.

Yield: depends on the size of popcorn balls

POPCORN SNACK

This is an imitation of a commercial product widely available, but made with sugar. But if you want a prize in the bottom of the bowl, you'll have to add it yourself.

The honey taste is intended to be much more noticeable in this snack than in *Popcorn Balls*.

½ popped recipe Salt-Free Popcorn *(see above)*	*1 cup shelled peanuts (with skins)* *½ cup honey*

Pour the popped corn into a large bowl.

Add the peanuts and mix well.

In a small saucepan, bring the honey to a boil and simmer for 10 minutes over very low heat. Then pour the honey over the peanut-popcorn mixture.

Toss very well with a pair of forks, being careful not to let the honey collect at the bottom of the bowl (this hardens more quickly and becomes useless).

When cooled just enough to handle, press into small clumps by hand, and place on a clean dish. No need to wrap.

Yield: about 1½ quarts

POTATO ROUNDS

In our eternal quest for something to replace potato chips (there are few things worse for you), we were experimenting and came up with something not at all like chips, but very like potato. This is delicious in its own right (and, meanwhile, we continue the search).

1 pound potatoes, cooked	*1 teaspoon fennel seed*
1 teaspoon salt	*1 small (2 ounce) onion,*
scant cup whole wheat flour	*diced*

Mix all the ingredients together well and knead gently until smooth.

Pinch off handfuls of the dough and roll into sausage shapes about 1 inch thick.

Slice into pellets less than ¼ inch thick and place on a greased baking sheet (see chapter on "Greasing without Grease").

Sprinkle the tops with a variety of herbs: some with poppy seeds, or powdered garlic, or basil, etc.

Broil about 20 minutes, at high heat.

Yield: many dozens

14

Fruit Desserts

The best and most desirable fruit desserts, are, simply, fresh fruit—fresh off the tree or vine, unsprayed, unshipped, untampered with. Unfortunately, most of you reading this book don't live in the fruit-growing centers.

Next best, then, is fresh fruit that *has* been shipped.

Fruit begins to lose its flavor and vitamin content as soon as it is picked (except for those fruits, such as bananas and some oranges, picked green and ripened on the way to market). So, often, the fruit we have to choose from in a market is not at its vitamin richest and certainly not at its most flavorful by the time we buy it.

If you can't get good fresh fruit to eat as is, then read on, because these recipes can bring the flavor back to that unflavorful fruit.

Fruit that is as fresh as you can get it is preferred for these recipes. Canned fruit is taboo, because the canning process destroys vitamins, as well as adding sweeteners, preservatives, and sometimes salt. There is some vitamin loss in the freezing process, too, but frozen is an acceptable substitute when and where fresh is unobtainable.

For many cooked-fruit desserts, see the "Puddings" chapter.

RIPOFF(APPLE)SAUCE

This is our favorite camping or hosteling dessert. And it has a history.

While traveling through Pennsylvania, Maryland, and West Virginia by bike one year, we came to an area where no stores were open on a Sunday. All we had in our bicycle saddlebags to eat were a lemon and some milk powder, a little honey, and some herb tea (we never travel without honey and herb tea).

We passed a deserted orchard on our way to our hostel. It was really in bad shape: there wasn't a sound apple to be found on the ground or on the trees. But we picked as many as we could carry, because, after all, we'd been out all day. After we had salvaged enough apple chunks for a pot of applesauce we reached the moment of truth: we could put honey in the applesauce, or we could have it in our herb tea.

We opted for a honeyless sauce, and honeyed tea, putting the lemon in the sauce.

And we never tasted a better applesauce. So, in memory of the day we discovered you don't need honey or any sweetener for a fruit sauce, we named the recipe Ripoff Sauce (to commemorate our ripping off the apples).

Depending on which orchard you rip off, *Ripoff Pear Sauce* and *Ripoff Peach Sauce* both work marvelously well with the same technique. It's strange, but the fruit seems to sweeten as you cook it.

Leave on as much of the skins as you can.

3 pound apples more or less *(after coring and trimming, but with skins)*	**1** small lemon **½** cup water

Put apples into a large pot.

Wash and pit the lemon, and slice rather thin, with skin on. Add to apples.

Add the water, and cook everything over medium heat for 20 to 25 minutes. Mash to the desired texture with a potato masher.

Taste the sauce and, if absolutely necessary, add a tablespoon or two of honey.

Yield: about 5 cups

PEAR COMPOTE

Here's a more civilized and sweeter cooked fruit. It's especially appropriate for those times of year when *all* the fruit seems to come into market too green to enjoy.

2 pounds pears	2 tablespoons honey
1 small lemon	

Wash and core, but do not peel, the pears. Cut them into eighths, and put them into a 4-quart pot.

Scrub the lemon and pit, but don't peel it, then cut it into ⅛-inch slices. Add to the pears.

Spoon in the honey, stir, bring to the boil over medium heat, then cook uncovered for about 20 minutes.

Yield: about 1 quart of compote

CHUNKY PEAR SAUCE

Do you live alone? Here's a small recipe, just for you (or for you and a friend with a light appetite).

Because this dish calls for so much honey, you must cook it at a simmer. Otherwise, it just won't keep the light color.

We like to serve this sweet dessert with fresh cold yoghurt. The combination of cold tart yoghurt and hot sweet pears is a real winner.

¾ pound pears	½ cup honey

Pit and stem the pears, but leave their skins on, and cut them into ½- to ¾-inch chunks.

Add the honey and simmer for about 35 minutes (stirring

only as you must to prevent scorching) or until the honey thickens and begins to darken.

Yield: 1 cup

STRAWBERRY FLUFF

This delightful dessert is a marvelous company dish and one the kids will love too (as well as being rich in protein and vitamin A). However, it does take time to prepare and requires chilling time.

1 pint fresh strawberries	½ cup cold water
1 small lemon	2 teaspoons vanilla extract
½ cup honey	1 cup ice water
1 tablespoon unflavored gelatin	1 cup instant milk powder

Put a large bowl and your beaters into the refrigerator to chill.

Wash, drain, and dice the berries into a medium mixing bowl.

Wash, peel, and pit the lemon, then liquefy it in a blender or mill. Add to the berries.

Measure in the honey and mix very well. Set the mixture into your freezer to chill for one hour.

In the top of a double boiler, mix together the gelatin and the ½ cup cold water. Set over the bottom of the boiler, put on the top of the stove at a simmer until the gelatin dissolves (the water will clear). Remove from the heat and allow to cool for 5 minutes.

Remove the berry mixture from the freezer, stir in the gelatin, add the vanilla extract, stir very well, and return to the freezer.

In the chilled bowl and with the chilled beaters, beat together the ice water and milk powder until stiff (about 10 to 15 minutes). While beating, stir occasionally.

Remove the berry mixture from the freezer and stir it well into the bowlful of whipped milk.

Serve immediately or allow to set further in the freezer.

Yield: 6 servings

LEMON FLUFF

Here's another way to get a very fluffy dessert.

4 large egg yolks (see
  "Separating Eggs" in
  "Cakes" chapter)
1 large lemon
3 tablespoons honey

1 cup ice water
1 cup instant milk powder
2 tablespoons honey
  (additional)

Put a large bowl and beaters into the refrigerator to chill.

Put the yolks into a medium mixing bowl.

Wash and pit, but don't peel, the lemon, then liquefy pulp and skin together in a blender. Add to the yolks.

Measure the honey into the lemon-yolk mixture and beat until frothy.

Pour the mixture into the top of a double boiler. Set the top over the bottom of the double boiler and cook over medium-low heat until very thick—about 20 minutes. When thick, remove from the heat and allow to cool.

In the chilled bowl, beat up the ice water and milk powder until half stiff, then drip in the honey, and beat until quite stiff—about 15 minutes.

In a serving bowl, mix together the cooled eggs and the beaten milk, until quite smooth. Serve immediately.

Yield: about 6 servings

COLD AND QUICK PAPAYA PUDDING

This makes up very fast, and it is delightful. It's necessary to use frozen fruit for this dessert.

1¼ *pounds frozen organic*   ¾   *cup honey*
   papaya (1 package)

Separate the frozen chunks of fruit, then put them in your blender.

Add the honey, and process until smooth. You'll have to shut off the motor and stir frequently.

Scrape out of the blender and serve.

Yield: about 6 servings

15

Miscellany

This chapter contains some of the most unusual and interesting dishes in the book—recipes that are referred to in other chapters, recipes that we hope you won't skip just because they're so far back in the book.

PIZZA DOUGH

(All-Purpose Dough)

Here is a yeast dough made up like any other yeast dough, but this one is specially flavored for pizza or bread sticks.

If you don't find these herbs to your taste, by all means substitute others. However, don't leave the herbs out completely unless you expect to bake the dough as a loaf of bread.

1 teaspoon fennel seed	1 tablespoon salt
2 tablespoons active dry yeast	3¾ to 4 cups whole wheat flour
2 cups warm tap water (or warm vegetable water)	½ teaspoon oil for bowl
3 tablespoons dried oregano	3 tablespoons unsaturated vegetable oil (1 per pizza) (optional)

Into a large bowl, measure the fennel, yeast, water, oregano, and salt. Stir.

Stir in 2 cups of flour until all wet. Add another cup of flour and mix in well.

Place ½ cup flour onto a kneading surface and place the batter on it. Mix flour into batter.

Add as much additional flour (¼ to ½ cup) as you need to make a kneadable but soft dough. Knead with your palms and the flats of your fingers. Don't dig your fingers into the dough or they will stick and you'll have to add more flour.

Knead for from 5 to 10 minutes, or until the dough is very cohesive and rather resilient. If you pick up the dough with one hand and turn it over, it will tend to fall all together, rather than breaking up. Also, if you poke the dough with a few fingers, it will fill in the holes.

Scrape down the same bowl you used before, pour in the ½ teaspoon of oil, and set the ball of dough back in the bowl. Turn the dough several times to coat it with the oil.

Cover with a clean, damp towel and set in a warm place (under 140°) to rise for about 1½ hours, or until sufficiently risen.

Rising and a test for sufficient rising isn't as important for pizza dough as it is with bread. Pizza dough doesn't have to rise as much.

When the dough is risen considerably, punch it down and knead out as many bubbles as you can.

Divide into 3 parts. Each part will make one pizza.

Preheat your oven to 400° to 450°.

At this stage you must decide whether you want an oily dough or not. The oil makes for a better flavor, but it is high in calories.

For an oily dough, simply add 1 tablespoon of unsaturated vegetable oil to each third of dough. Knead oil in well.

If you're not adding oil to the dough, oil your baking sheet lightly. (We don't own a round sheet; instead we use a large rectangular one.)

On a clean surface, roll out the ⅓ of dough to approximately the size and shape of your baking sheet. Place dough on the sheet and trim off any excess (or patch any short places). If you have difficulty rolling the dough to size, flatten it as best you can, then place it on the sheet and spread it by poking it with stiff fingers.

Set the tray in the preheated oven (*without topping—that comes later*). Bake for approximately 10 minutes, or until browned and crisp.

Remove from the oven briefly, top with your favorite *Pizza Topping* (see below), sprinkle with grated Parmesan, or crumbled mozzarella cheese, and return to the oven for a few minutes, until the cheese melts and the topping is hot.

The best idea is to time your topping so that it is *hot* when it goes on top of the *Pizza Dough*.

Repeat for other 2 parts of dough.

Yield: 3 pizza shells

Note:

This dough can be stored, covered, in the refrigerator for 3 or 4 days, and it may be frozen for months.

PIZZA TOPPING

We promise not to tell if you decide to use this recipe as a vegetable side dish instead of *Pizza Topping*.

1	tablespoon unsaturated vegetable oil (for the skillet)	1	medium clove garlic (or 2 teaspoons garlic powder)
2	pounds ripe tomatoes	1	tablespoon granulated kelp
1½	teaspoons salt		
1	tablespoon dried basil	¼	cup grated Parmesan cheese or crumbled mozzarella
2	teaspoons dried oregano		

Oil a large skillet.

Wash and trim the tomatoes (don't skin them) and cut them into sixteenths. Place them in the skillet.

Add the salt, basil, oregano, and garlic. Cook over a high heat until mixture is thickish, about 7 minutes. When the tomatoes are soft, mash them in the skillet, with a slotted spoon.

Remove mixture from the heat. Stir in the kelp.

Pour the topping, while still hot, over the hot *Pizza Dough* (see above).

Sprinkle pizza with the grated cheese. Return to the oven for a few minutes, until the cheese melts.

Yield: topping for 1 large pizza.

SOFT PRETZELS

Have you ever been to the Pennsylvania Dutch country? Then you've perhaps tasted one of their specialties—those soft pretzels. We love them, but most recipes for them call for lye. Lye isn't added to the dough, but the pretzels are boiled in a bit of it to get that shiny look. Well, we can do without the shine and without the lye.

Don't be put off by the involved directions—these treats really are worth the extra effort.

1	teaspoon salt	2	tablespoons honey
1	tablespoon active dry yeast	1½	cups whole wheat flour
1	cup hot tap water	1	teaspoon baking soda
⅓	cup instant milk powder	½	cup fresh yoghurt
¼	cup unsaturated vegetable oil	1½	cups whole wheat flour (additional)

Optional Flavorings
caraway seeds
poppy seeds

onion flakes
powdered garlic
coarse salt

In a large bowl, mix the first 7 ingredients together very well.

Cover with a clean, damp towel. Set in a warm place for ½ to 1 hour, or until you can see good bubble activity.

Remove mixture from the warm place and stir.

Add the baking soda, yoghurt, and the additional 1½ cups of flour. Knead it for 5 to 10 minutes into a very light but cohesive dough.

Set to rise again in a warm place, for 1½ to 2 hours, until quite well risen.

Knead down.

Divide the dough into 10 roughly equal pieces.

Roll a piece into a long snake, about 20 inches by ½ inch, then twist into an overhand knot or into a pretzel shape. Place twisted pretzel on a clean surface.

Repeat until all pretzels are twisted.

Simmer a few inches of water in the bottom of a small Dutch oven or a very wide pot.

Lightly grease two large baking sheets (see "Greasing without Grease" chapter).

Lift a raw pretzel with a slotted pancake turner. Dip it into the barely-simmering water. Allow it to stay under the water for only a few seconds.

Remove pretzel from the water, drain for a few seconds, then lay it on a greased baking sheet.

Repeat, leaving room between each pretzel for some spreading, until you have a trayful.

Then sprinkle the tops of the wet pretzels with optional coatings: caraway seeds, poppy seeds, onion flakes, powdered garlic—even coarse salt, if you must.

Fill the other baking sheet similarly.

Starting in a cold oven, bake at medium-high (about 375°), 20 to 30 minutes, until quite brown.

Yield: 10 large pretzels

EGGPLANT DIP

Something special for your next social gathering—coming to us by way of Israel.

Make certain the eggplant is really soft before you remove it from the oven, or your dip won't come out smooth.

2 medium eggplants	½ teaspoon salt, to taste
1 small lemon	pepper, to taste
¼ cup safflower seed oil	

Wash, trim, and halve the eggplants lengthwise. Lay them flat-side down on a large, ungreased baking sheet.

Bake at medium-high (about 375°) for 35 to 40 minutes, or until the eggplant meat is *very* soft. Remove from the oven.

When the eggplants have cooled, scrape the soft flesh into your blender. Discard the skins.

Wash, peel, and pit the lemon. Add it to the eggplant in the blender, and blend until smooth.

Gradually drip the oil into blender as you reblend until smooth.

Taste for salt and pepper.

Yield: almost 1 quart

FISH FILLING

This dish was invented especially to fill *Whole Wheat Puffs* (see "Pastries and Pie Crusts" chapter), but it can also be used as a canapé topping with any of our cracker recipes or as a crêpes filling. (To fill crêpes, double the recipe. For crêpes recipes, see our book, *Blend It Splendid*.)

Frozen fish is not quite as good nutritionally as fresh fish. However, unless you can get fish fresh from the water, stick to frozen. The "fresh" fish we can get at our fish stores is often anything but fresh.

If you do use fresh instead of frozen, cook it very little and oil the skillet lightly.

½ *pound fish fillet, frozen solid*
¼ *teaspoon dill seed*
paprika, to taste

¼ *teaspoon salt, to taste*
2 *tablespoons unsaturated vegetable oil*

Cut the fish into ½-inch cubes with a serrated knife.

Place fish in a large *ungreased* skillet. Add the dill seed. Cook at medium temperature, stirring frequently. Don't overcook the fish: there should be no raw spots, but when the raw spots disappear, remove from heat.

Add the paprika and salt to taste.

Scrape mixture into a large bowl and mash in only enough oil to make a thick paste.

Yield: enough filling for 1 *Whole Wheat Puffs* recipe.

CHESTNUT CREAM

Like chestnuts? We love them. Here's a recipe that can be eaten as a sweet by itself, or with a bit of yoghurt, or even used as a cake filling or topping.

2 *pounds fresh chestnuts*	2 *tablespoons instant*
¾ *cup honey (or more)*	*milk powder*
1 *tablespoon vanilla extract*	

Peel the hard outer shell from the chestnuts as best you can.

Place chestnuts in a 3-quart pot and cover with water. Boil briskly for 15 minutes until the chestnuts are soft, but not mushy.

Remove chestnuts from heat, allow to cool somewhat, and peel off the inner skins. These skins should come off easily.

In a sturdy bowl, mash the chestnuts with a potato masher.

Place honey in a small saucepan and heat just to boiling. Add honey to the chestnuts and mash until pureed.

Add the vanilla and milk powder. Mash until very, very smooth.

Taste for the possible addition of more honey.

If the mixture is too thick, thin with a little milk or water. Serve as described above, or as a crêpes filling or in a *Tart Shell* (see "Pastries and Pie Crusts" chapter) topped by *Whipped Topping* or *Creme Chantilly* (see below).

Yield: about 3 cups

CREME CHANTILLY

Here is a French dessert cream. It's made with powdered nonfat milk and will hold its body beautifully.

Eat it as it is, or as a topping, or a filling for *Eclairs* (see "Pastries and Pie Crusts" chapter), or mix it with fresh fruit. It is quite versatile.

¼	cup cold water	1	egg white (see "Separating Eggs" in "Cakes" chapter)
1½	teaspoons unflavored gelatin		
3	tablespoons honey	1½	cups noninstant milk powder
1½	cups ice water	1½	teaspoons vanilla extract

Set a large bowl and your beaters in the refrigerator to chill for about 15 minutes.

Measure the first 3 ingredients into the top of a double boiler. Mix well, then heat over simmering water until the gel and the honey are well dissolved.

Remove the gel mixture from the heat and allow to cool, but don't let it get cold enough to set.

In the chilled bowl, beat an egg white until just frothy.

Add the water and milk powder. Beat until almost stiff, about 10 minutes. Stir several times.

Beat in the vanilla and the gelatin mixture. Continue to beat until very stiff.

Serve at once or store for a day in the refrigerator.

Yield: about 6 cups

WHIPPED TOPPING

We have never been able to get *Whipped Topping* as stiff as whipped cream without the help of egg whites. If this recipe doesn't come out stiff enough for you, beat 2 egg whites in the chilled bowl until almost firm, then add the water and milk powder, and you'll get a stiffer topping.

However, if you don't need a very stiff topping, this

recipe works fine. Also, if you wish, you can set the *Whipped Topping* in the freezer where it will stiffen further and keep its shape.

Don't forget to chill your beaters and bowl very well. Make certain your water is ice water: the cold helps in the whipping. You just can't whip milk powder in a warm bowl or with warm water. At least we can't.

You may substitute 1 cup of noninstant milk powder for the instant milk powder.

1 cup instant milk powder   **2 tablespoons** Maple Sugar
1 cup ice water   *(optional) (see below)*
2 teaspoons vanilla extract

Chill a mixing bowl and beaters well, 15 to 30 minutes.

Into the chilled bowl, measure the milk powder and ice water. Beat, stirring occasionally, until half stiff.

Beat in the vanilla extract, then taste. If you wish, add *Maple Sugar* to taste and beat until stiff. Total beating time will be about 20 minutes.

Yield: 12 servings

MAPLE SUGAR

Here's a dry sugar which is actually healthy—mineral-rich, in fact. We simply boil off the water from maple syrup. To make this sugar "granulated," we grind it in the blender or mash it in a mortar and pestle to get it as fine as we can. Then we use it in icings, in *Whipped Topping* (see above) or in any recipe that calls for sugar.

1 cup maple syrup

Simmer the maple syrup for 25 to 30 minutes on low heat. Stir frequently (especially toward the end of the cooking) until the resulting "foam" (that's what it looks like) is *very* thick.

Immediately pour into an ungreased soup bowl. The "foam" should not collapse.

When sugar has cooled, break it up and grind fine in a blender, a quarter of the yield at a time, or crush with a mortar and pestle. If the sugar stays too liquid to grind, scrape it back into the pot and cook for a few more minutes.

Store in covered container. *Stores very well.*

Yield: 1 cup

STRAWBERRY SAUCE

Maybe the fresh, early-in-the-season strawberries you can get are so tart that you feel they are unusable. Try them here.

This sauce is too liquid to be a cake filling or icing, but it makes a lovely drench over a plain cake or as a topping for ice cream.

1 pint fresh strawberries	*¼ cup plus 1 tablespoon honey*

Puree the berries in your blender.

Add the honey and mix again until smooth.

Serve at once or store in the fridge (but for no more than a day or so; this is not a keeper).

Yield: about 2 cups

TOMATO KETCHUP

Since we use no colorings or color preservers, our ketchup darkens in the cooking. The flavor, however, is excellent. And it doesn't matter whether you use the most expensive tomatoes or the cheapest. After cooking, they're pretty much the same.

5 pounds ripe tomatoes	3 teaspoons ground cloves
½ cup wine vinegar	(optional)
½ cup honey	1 to 3 teaspoons granulated
2 teaspoons salt	kelp, to taste

Wash and core the tomatoes. Squeeze out most of their juice and seeds. (Save the juice to drink.) Cut tomatoes into chunks and put the chunks into a 6-quart pot.

Add the vinegar, honey, salt, and the cloves if you wish.

Cook over low heat for about 1½ hours, stirring frequently.

When the mixture thickens, remove it from the heat. Stir in the granulated kelp, to taste.

Store in the refrigerator in glass jars.

Yield: about 4 cups

TEN MINUTE CRANBERRY RELISH

This is our preferred ketchup for as many months of the year as we can get fresh cranberries or have any cranberries left in our freezer.

It makes up in only 10 minutes and it doesn't lose any flavor because it's cooked so little.

¾ cup honey	1 teaspoon ground
2 _tomatoes (about	cinnamon
½ pound)	½ teaspoon salt
1 teaspoon ground cloves	1 pound whole fresh
	cranberries (or thawed)

Measure the honey into a 3-quart pot.

Wash, core, and chunk the tomatoes. Add them to the pot.

Add the cloves, cinnamon, and salt. Cook over medium heat, uncovered, for about 5 minutes.

Wash the berries in hot water and pick out any stems or bad berries.

Add berries to the honey mixture and stir well.

Cook for 5 additional minutes over medium heat, uncovered, then mash all the berries with a slotted spoon or fine potato masher.

Mix well and remove from the heat.

Store in the fridge in glass jars. Keeps well.

Yield: about 2½ cups

SWEET CRANBERRY RELISH

1¼ cups honey	1 teaspoon ground cloves
2 apples	1 teaspoon ground
1 pound whole fresh	cinnamon
cranberries (or thawed)	½ teaspoon powdered
½ teaspoon salt	ginger

Measure the honey into a 3-quart pot.

Scrub the apples and core them, but do not peel. Dice the apples, and add them to the honey.

Wash the berries in hot water and pick out any stems or bad berries. Add to the pot.

Add the remaining ingredients and cook over medium heat for about 10 minutes.

Mash with a potato masher or slotted spoon, and cook for 5 more minutes.

Mix very well, then remove from the heat.

Store in glass jars in the fridge. Keeps well.

Yield: about 3 cups

CABBAGE KNISHES

We know full well that knishes are supposed to be rolled in dough, not in cabbage leaves—but we couldn't resist this combination. The filling *is* a knish filling, and the outside of *these* knishes is cabbage leaves.

We have a bit of conflict here. The outermost, darkest-green leaves of the cabbage are the most nutritious. But they are also the toughest. For this recipe we want leaves that have some flexibility in them, leaves that will hold the filling in, but will not fight back when you bite into them. So, we say this: use the paler—but still large—inner leaves for this recipe, and save the outermost leaves for a wholesome and tasty cabbage soup.

12 to 14 large cabbage leaves	¾ teaspoon fennel seed
1½ pounds cooked potatoes (still hot)	3 teaspoons dried onion
	salt and pepper, to taste
6 ounces uncolored mild cheese	

Set a large pot of lightly salted water to boil.

Cut the thick midrib from each cabbage leaf, and cut in half along that central rib. Put the leaf halves into the boiling water, bring back to the boil. Cook for 5 minutes.

Remove pot from the heat and drain. (The water can be the start of that soup we were talking about.)

Set the leaf halves out on a plate, stacking them like pancakes. (Handle with blunt tongs or a pair of spoons to protect both you and the leaves—they mustn't be punctured and you mustn't be burned.)

Mash the warm potatoes in a mixing bowl.

Grate the cheese in. Add the rest of the ingredients. Mix very well, then taste for salt and pepper.

Spoon about 2 tablespoonfuls of the filling onto the middle of a leaf. Fold the leaf over the filling like an envelope: bring the bottom up and over, fold the sides in, then fold the top down.

Pull the rolled knish into an 8- by 12-inch oven-proof dish (ungreased).

Spoon filling onto the next leaf, and repeat until all the leaves are rolled up and in the dish. This should fill the dish.

The exact amount of filling you use will depend on the size of the leaf. You want to wind up with a knish about 1 inch thick and about 3 inches long. But if your leaves are very large or small, you'll have to adjust the amount of filling. If that first knish looks too small, use more filling on the next. If the first looks like the potato is bursting out, take some filling away and reroll.

When all the knishes are in the dish, set the dish under the broiler for about 15 minutes at high temperature. Be careful: scorched cabbage is bitter. You want to heat the knishes and brown them slightly on top, not burn them.

Yield: 24 to 28

Crudités

Finger foods are an important part of our diet and our most frequent finger foods are *"crudités"*—another French word, translatable as "raws."

Crudités are any of a great number of vegetables eaten raw: carrot or cucumber sticks, cauliflower or broccoli tips, celery or radishes or Chinese cabbage—many common and not-so-common vegetables that you can eat as they are (washed and chilled), or dipped into a dip (see the Israeli *Eggplant Dip,* page 208), or mayonnaise (see our book, *Blend It Splendid,* Rodale Press, 1973, for several).

Crudités should always be the freshest of vegetables, the crispest, the nearest to the vine. You may be able to get away with last week's broccoli cooked, *but never raw.*

Do use these best of *hors d'oeuvres* with any meal, as well as our fancier recipes for special occasions.

16

Greasing Without Grease

We no longer grease our baking pans or sheets or anything that goes into the oven, at least not with anything you'd recognize as "grease." Butter has too much fat, margarine has too many chemicals, and unsaturated oils, while usually safe, are often not "greasy" enough for baking or for things that must stay in the oven for more than a few minutes. Besides, oil often does leave a greasy residue on foods. This residue can go rancid after a short while if the food is not refrigerated.

For a time, in our search for a "grease" both effective and healthy, we were using beeswax, which has a delightful scent while it's cooking. We would rub a brick of beeswax over the surface to be "greased," and often it worked very well. Sometimes, however, it was difficult to get into corners with the brick. Sometimes we would be careless and miss a spot and whatever we were baking would stick. Sometimes we left too much on and got the taste of wax in the food (a nice taste, but wax all the same).

What we use now is called "liquid lecithin." Lecithin is a very stable oil extracted from soybeans. It is rich in two B vitamins, choline and inositol. In addition to helping to dissolve cholesterol in your bloodstream, it makes everything you cook on act as if it were Teflon® coated. (We won't cook on Teflon®—you eat some of that coating with every meal.) Yes, liquid lecithin is the best "grease" we've ever used. Best of all, it doesn't leave things greasy.

We are not the only ones to recognize the virtues of lecithin. There is a commercial product on the market called "Pam®." It contains liquid lecithin and a "propellant." We won't eat any "propellants" or breathe any aerosols, and we won't stand for the expense of this sort of packaging.

Our bottles of lecithin are marked "unrefined." The stuff looks terrible, rather like the heaviest grade of crankcase oil. But don't be put off by the looks. It has a slight scent too, but no flavor at all after it's been used in cooking.

To grease with lecithin, pour out the smallest amount you can and, with your fingers and palm, spread it over the cooking surface of whatever baking sheet or pan you're using. Stop the lecithin at the lip of the jar with your finger. A bit the size of a thin dime will "grease" a large baking sheet. For most recipes, even the thinnest, barest layer is enough to grease without sticking.

This spreading technique leaves some of the lecithin on your hand. Great! Rub it in as if it were a hand cream, then wash it off well with soap and water. Even after washing, your hands will be left smoother. This is really remarkable stuff!

Also, lecithin is cheap. As of this writing, a pint costs about $1.15, but you need so little that it comes out to a fraction of a cent per greasing. Several batches of cookies can be baked on the same sheet without regreasing; just shake off the crumbs or gently wipe away any that won't shake off.

Finally, lecithined pans clean up *very* quickly. If you are the family's pot and pan washer, we don't have to tell you that a substance that cuts your pot-washing time by 90 percent is worth its weight in rubies.

You will have to go to a natural foods store to get unrefined liquid lecithin. We recommend it most highly for greasing without grease.

Ingredients

A Brief Dictionary of the Ingredients in Our Recipes

Our main source for the nutritional values of foods is a United States Department of Agriculture publication, Agriculture Handbook No. 8, *Composition of Foods*. This thick handbook is the single most valuable food book in our library. It can be ordered from:

> *Superintendent of Documents*
> *U. S. Government Printing Office*
> *Washington, D.C. 20402*

The current price is $2.00 per copy, plus postage. If you wish to order it in bulk, for a school or co-op or the like, you can get a discount. However, you'll have to write to the above address for details.

When it comes to chemicals in food, the U. S. Department of Agriculture has a list of food additives that are Generally Regarded As Safe. This is the so-called GRAS List (pronounced "grass"). The food processors, when confronted with a complaint about additives, always point to the GRAS List as their justification.

Two points we think you should keep in mind about this list: first of all, just because a chemical is listed as "safe" and legally *can* be added to a food doesn't mean that it *must* be added to a food. We sometimes wonder if food processors aren't more interested in keeping their chemists busy than in providing wholesome food.

Second, understand that the GRAS List is not writ in stone. Chemicals are frequently taken off because they turn out to be *un*safe, even as new, insufficiently-tested ones are added.

Arrowroot Starch

Arrowroot starch is the very-finely-ground tuberous root of various plants including the *maranta* (one species of which houseplant growers know as "prayer plant").

It has the same uses as cornstarch: thickening soups, puddings, sauces. However, with arrowroot you can get a much thicker result than you can with cornstarch (see our *Turkish Delight* in "Cooked Candies" chapter).

This is also a more desirable thickener than cornstarch because it is nutritionally superior and quite easily digested. Cornstarch is ground from the endosperm of the corn kernel—the starchy inner part without the germ or the bran. This makes it literally starch, 90 percent carbohydrate with virtually no vitamins or minerals.

Arrowroot, on the other hand, coming as it does from a root and not from a grain, does contain vitamins and minerals, although it is still high in carbohydrates.

Artichoke Noodles

The artichoke noodles we use are made from durham wheat, soy flour, and ground Jerusalem or American artichokes. Jerusalem artichokes are tubers and no relation to the globe-shaped variety of artichoke that you eat leaf by green leaf down to the solid heart.

Artichoke noodles offer good quality protein (from the soy flour). They also give you a wide range of minerals—the kinds of minerals that only root vegetables seem to yield. Organic whole wheat noodles contain higher concentrations of vitamins, but artichoke noodles are richer in minerals.

As an aside, did you know that Jerusalem artichokes

are among the easiest vegetables to grow? And that their calorie content varies according to their freshness? Just harvested, they have as few as 22 calories per pound (celery has 58 calories per pound). Stored for a long period of time (they can be stored as turnips are), these tubers might contain up to 235 calories per pound—which is still fairly low.

Baking Soda

Baking soda is the common name for the mineral compound known as sodium bicarbonate (bicarbonate of soda). This is a sodium compound and should really be avoided by anyone on a sodium-restricted diet. Baking soda is not the same as baking powder, which can contain aluminum sulfate, monocalcium phosphate monohydrate, calcium carbonate, calcium sulfate, tartaric acid, and other chemical compounds we consider undesirable.

Baking powder acts as a leavening agent by releasing bubbles in the presence of water or heat and water. Baking soda releases the necessary bubbles only in the presence of an acid (such as yoghurt or sour milk).

Neither has any nutritional value.

The major difference between the two is that some of the compounds in baking powder accumulate in the body, while the compound that is baking soda is easily eliminated.

Bicarb (baking soda) is used medicinally as a neutralizer for so-called "excess stomach acid," a highly dubious practice. Now, we aren't doctors, but it is clear that the stomach must have its acids to work. If you neutralize your stomach acids, you cannot digest your foods. So we never use bicarb or any other alkalizer, medicinally.

In our recipes, we use only as much soda as will be neutralized *before* it gets to the stomach. Therefore, as an alkalizer it has no effect on our system.

Baking powder we never use at all. Even after it has worked fully and released all its bubbles it is still an undesirable compound.

Beans

If the world continues in its present direction, beans will undoubtedly become an increasingly important source of supplementary (and primary) protein.

Ecologically, beans are way ahead of animal protein sources. They can provide high quality protein without the wastes created by the animal proteins. Beans do not add pollutants to the biosphere as the great cattle herds do. Although beans may be grown nonorganically and sprayed, they are never injected with antibiotics and hormones. Also, organically-raised beans are much more readily available than is organically-raised beef. Dollar for dollar, beans are a better protein buy.

In our recipes we call for black-eyed peas (also known as cowpeas), chick peas (also known as garbanzos), and soybeans. (Many vegetables called peas are actually beans). Of these, soybeans are undoubtedly the best, nutritionally. They contain the most protein of any bean, as well as the most complete protein. Served as a *Soy crunch* (see "Snacks" chapter), they make a protein supplement that you and your children can carry about and munch on.

Beans are also among the best sources of potassium you can find—a fact not to be ignored in the high-sodium world we live in. As we say elsewhere, a "potassium-rich food, who can value? For its worth is above rubies." To translate: it is very easy to find lots of sodium (and with it, lots of circulatory problems) if one indulges in a processed-foods diet. It is much more difficult to find potassium-rich foods, like beans, to balance out the undesirable consequences of that sodium.

Butter

Don't kid yourself. Butter is more than 95 percent fat, with more than 3,000 calories per pound, or about 100 calories per tablespoon. Margarine is only about 80 percent fat, but contains the same amount of calories.

But margarine is a stew of saturated vegetable oils, salt and chemicals, while sweet butter is pure cream. We don't use enough butter in our diet to worry about the fat. We're active and we eat balanced meals and take vitamin supplements: our bodies easily handle the fat we get from butter. The chemicals people get in margarine aren't so easy to handle.

Butter can be a very good source of vitamin A, but be warned that the vitamin A in butter comes from the grass the cows eat (that's where the yellow color comes from, too). In the winter, when the cows feed on grain, the vitamin A content of butter is much lower (and its yellow color is more likely to come from a dye).

We use only sweet butter because salting butter increases the sodium content by 100 times. Who needs that much salt?

Carob Flour

Carob flour is the ground-up dried fruit of the carob tree. The fruit is known also as Saint-John's bread. The flour does not include the seeds or the skin.

This flour is a dark tan in color and can be used as a chocolate substitute. It is virtually fat-free, compared with baking chocolate which is half fat. While carob is naturally sweet, it has only about ⅓ the calories of the baking chocolate.

Carob flour (or powder, as it is also known) can also be used mixed with milk for a "cocoa" drink. Carob powder has half the calories of cocoa powder and, again, much less fat.

Chocolate is a really bad baddie. *Many* people are allergic to it, it is high in calories and in fat, it is bad for complexions, and the oxalic acid in chocolate interferes with calcium absorption. Carob has none of these drawbacks and is itself an aid to digestion.

While carob is a chocolate substitute, it doesn't really, by itself, taste a lot like chocolate. In our recipes, we've played with it a little to bring the flavor closer.

Cheese

Cheese is an excellent source of complete protein and easy to digest.

The flavors of the various cheeses come from the techniques of their manufacture. Cheese *is* a processed food. There is no such thing as a *natural* cheese, aside from certain curdlings that milk may make on its own. Other flavoring influences are the milk, the animal whose milk is used, and the amount of salt.

What is called processed cheese is a set cheese that has been mixed with water, a "stabilizer," and perhaps a dye; then fillers, flavorings, and more salt; then reset.

We use only *uncolored* cheeses. Cream, from which cheese is processed, is at most a pale shade of yellow. Orange and bright yellow cheeses have been dyed, and dyes, no matter how "natural," have no place in our diet.

Do keep in mind that cheese and cheese products are "Standard of Identity" foods. Unless you get a so-called "diet" cheese (diet foods must have ingredients listed on the label), you won't be able to tell if your cheese is dyed or how much salt it contains (unless it's marked "salt-free").

There are unadulterated cheeses available, if you are willing to look for them. Try natural foods stores.

Coconut Shreds, Desiccated

To make coconut shreds, the meat of the coconut is first dried, then shredded into small bits. Coconut shreds make an excellent sweetener and add calcium, phosphorus, iron, potassium (*no* sodium), and even small amounts of the B vitamins to your diet.

Store in the refrigerator to keep the shreds from turning rancid.

Coffee

Stan was never a coffee drinker, but Floss drank as many as 10 to 12 cups a day when we were first married. Floss's waking up in the morning was like all the bad jokes about people who can't do anything but mumble and grump until they have their first cup of coffee.

That's no joke: caffeine *is* addictive, and confirmed coffee drinkers can't get going until they have their first caffeine "fix" of the day.

When we switched to tea, the change in Floss was remarkable. She actually began opening her eyes before breakfast and speaking in more pleasing tones and intelligible phrases than "glmp," and "argh."

Now we've switched to herb tea and both of us start the day just by opening our eyes—not with a cigarette, not with a cup of something with caffeine.

Decaffeinated coffees are superior to coffees with caffeine: the drug is missing. Instant coffees are superior to ground coffees: the oil one finds in ground coffees is largely removed from the instant kind. Coffee substitutes are *sometimes* superior to either, sometimes not. A coffee substitute made with scorched grain and sugar is not a wholesome food. Also, some of the coffee substitutes taste like nothing at all—not coffee, not anything but colored water.

If you have a coffee substitute that you like, use it in those recipes where it's appropriate.

For regular day in, day out drinking, however, we recommend that old Argentinian tea favorite, *yerba matê* (also known simply as *matê* tea).

Corn

In some of our recipes we call for *freshly-ground* cornmeal. We say it there, but it's important enough to say it again: corn keeps very well in the grain (berry), stored dry. Once you grind it, however, it loses the protective outer skin and starts to lose food value—and the oils in it start to turn rancid.

If you grind corn just before using it, fine. If you buy it already ground, you may be buying trouble. Store-bought cornmeal may have been stored out of the refrigerator, sitting in some warehouse, losing food value and turning rancid.

The germ has been removed from the bulk of commercial cornmeal. Why? The germ carries most of the oil and degerminating keeps the cornmeal from going rancid. Unfortunately, the germ also contains the bulk of corn's nutrients; degermination turns cornmeal into a devitalized food product.

We grind our own meal in our blender, 1 cup at a time. It grinds up easily.

If you must buy cornmeal, buy meal that is not degerminated and has been stored in a refrigerator.

Eggs

Eggs are good food, and don't let anyone tell you otherwise. They have a very high-quality, complete protein, and plenty of it. (One large egg contains about 20 percent of an adult's total daily protein need.) Eggs also offer a broad range of vitamins and minerals.

Don't be frightened of the cholesterol content. Egg yolks also contain lecithin, a B complex which naturally combats and breaks down cholesterol.

Extracts, Vanilla and Almond

Extracts are largely composed of alcohol. The oils of the vanilla beans or the almonds are dissolved in the alcohol, and you get the resulting flavoring.

The alcohol evaporates during cooking. In uncooked recipes, the alcohol (however little) *is* eaten. Look, we are neither teetotalers nor big drinkers. We take wine with dinner sometimes, but we don't drink to excess. Alcohol *is* a poison and a large amount does damage. Stay moderate.

You can purchase so-called organic extracts, though we don't believe there really is any organically-raised vanilla available. We use only small amounts of these extracts, and trust to our good constitutions and good diet to get us over any problems we just don't know about.

Fish

Fish is another complete protein food. It is even better than meat because it is low in saturated fats.

The main thing that worries us about fish is the growing pollution of fresh-water streams and even the oceans. There are some cleaner waters around Iceland and Greenland, and we try to get fish caught there. Freshness is another problem. We eat mostly frozen fish, fish which has been frozen aboard the ship that caught it.

If you can get fresh fish from unpolluted waters, great. For those of us who live far away from such places, frozen fish is the safest solution.

Fruit, Dried

Dried fruits are higher in calories per pound than the same fruits fresh. Evaporating the water in the drying process concentrates the calories, but it also concentrates the vitamins and minerals.

Dried apricots, especially, are a rich source of vitamin A, a vitamin often hard to come by in the winter months when the supply of green leafy vegetables can be short. But all the dried fruits we use supply iron, too, and a wide range of other nutrients.

But please don't overindulge when you eat these fruits as a snack. They are, as we said, high in calories. And just because you are eating a natural and organically-grown dried apricot doesn't mean you shouldn't brush your teeth or at least rinse your mouth afterwards. There is sugar, albeit fructose, in those fruits.

The major problem with dried fruits can be the chemicals used in their processing—sulfur, especially. Stan has had canker-sore reactions to these chemicals, and you may, too. So do get only natural, unsprayed, sun-dried, organically-raised dried fruits. They are widely available and well worth the price.

By the by, natural dried fruit often looks darker and drabber than the commercial kinds; the commercial processors *bleach* their dried fruits to get that pale and glossy color. They may look beautiful, but eating that bleaching chemical makes bad baddies out of these naturally good goodies.

Fruits, Fresh

We use many fresh fruits in our recipes. There isn't a fresh fruit that isn't nutritionally desirable. If nothing else, they provide enzymes available *only* in raw food. And, apart from an occasional salad, how much raw food do you eat a day?

If you have digestion difficulties, consider papaya. It is the source for an enzyme that aids enormously in digestion.

Strawberries, watermelons, yellow peaches, and yellow or orange melons are good sources of vitamin A. If you're blending them into a recipe, they should be eaten as soon as possible after blending because contact with the air breaks down vitamin A.

Generally speaking, citrus fruits should be eaten with a bit of the white middle rind. This rind contains the bioflavonoids, which help to cement the cells together.

The fresh fruit you use should be unsprayed and grown organically, with natural fertilizers. Sprayed fruit introduces pesticides into your system. By the way, *all* fruit imported from Mexico to the U. S. is sprayed—it's the law. We recently discovered that all produce brought into the Bronx Terminal Market in New York is sprayed routinely to prevent the possible spread of insect infestation. If you must eat sprayed fruit, some of our friends suggest that you wash it in a solution of ¼ cup vinegar to 1 gallon of water, and then rinse very well. They say this will remove up to eighty percent of the pesticide residues.

Garlic

Only fresh garlic has the oil (no jokes about vampires please); the dried garlic flakes or the powdered garlic hasn't enough oil left in it to keep away even a baby vampire (ouch!). You can buy garlic oil separately in health food stores, not as a condiment but as a food supplement.

The dried garlic powder is much easier to store and to measure than is the fresh, and it doesn't add anything wet to an otherwise dry recipe. We know that for nutrition and for flavor the fresh is superior, but for the small amounts we use, we feel we can sometimes get away with the dry.

Gelatin, Unflavored

Gelatin is more than 85 percent protein, but it is an incomplete protein. If you can get the missing amino acids at the same meal, you can indeed increase your protein intake with a gelatin dessert.

Herbs and Spices

What is the difference between an herb and a spice? Generally speaking, herbs provide flavor without heat on the tongue, without bite. Spices bite.

Spices are irritants. Anyone suffering from hemorrhoids who goes and eats ginger can tell you that. Small amounts of spice are permissible in a well-balanced diet, for a person in good health. But someone with a glandular disorder may well find himself or herself reacting adversely to spices.

Fifteen years ago, Stan could run a fever from using too much pepper. Today, with his glands in better shape, we still use very little pepper. Instead, we use lots of herbs. Sage, for example, is not only terrific in recipes that should call for pepper, it is also an herb noted as a help to digestion.

Hardly anyone reacts adversely to herbs. In fact, for thousands of years herbs were the only medicine that humanity had. To this day herbs are used as tonics and folk remedies in many cultures.

Honey

Honey is more than 82 percent carbohydrate, compared with most processed sugars, which are over 99 percent carbohydrate. Even maple syrup is 90 percent carbohydrate. Honey also contains a little bit of protein, largely from the pollen that sneaks in, and small amounts of several vitamins and minerals.

It is very easily digested. Because your body processes honey rapidly, a honey-treat can be a source of energy soon after it is eaten.

Honey has an interesting flavor of its own (or rather many interesting flavors, depending on the flowers the bees have gathered the nectar from), but it also brings out the flavors of other foods.

As a food, there is no respect in which honey is not superior to granulated sugar. Even in terms of cavities, the molecules are much larger than cane and beet sugar molecules, and so the honey tends to sit on the surface of the tooth, and is less likely to cause cavities.

Honey is also less likely to cause the dependence that kids find today in addictive sugared soft drinks.

Honey is less likely than sugar to be a villain in heart disease.

All in all, why would anyone eat processed cane or beet sugars when they might have honey?

It is our favorite sweetener, and we use it in tea, in cooking, and in the making of many recipes in this book.

Kelp, Granulated

Kelp is a variety of seaweed. It is available in dried sheets or, less expensively, by weight, ground into a fine powder. We use it as a source of iodine, which everyone must have.

Floss was on thyroid tablets for years because her thyroid gland was not manufacturing enough thyroxin on its own. In our attempt to get away from doctors and from medication, Floss switched to granulated kelp (about 1 teaspoon per day). Kelp's iodine stimulates the thyroid. Floss takes the kelp sprinkled on food as if it were a condiment, or mixed into a liquefied tomato or cucumber. She has been on the seaweed for about three years; her thyroid level now tests as normal.

In addition to iodine, kelp also contains a remarkable amount of calcium (as much by weight as powdered skim milk). Of course, it contains a lot of sodium, and is therefore bad for anyone on a sodium-restricted diet. However, kelp's high potassium content tends to counterbalance the sodium somewhat.

Lecithin

Lecithin is an inexpensive emulsifier. Commercial candy-makers have long used it. Lecithin takes a layer of fatty stuff and breaks the fat down into smaller particles. It can do the same thing to the cholesterol in your bloodstream.

Basically, lecithin is composed of two B vitamins, choline and inositol. Lecithin is found naturally in egg yolks and soybeans. Commercial lecithin, taken from soybeans, is available in liquid or granular form. We use both.

We use the liquid lecithin, which looks like a particularly viscous grade of lubricating oil, in many recipes instead of butter as a grease for our baking pans and sheets. It has no taste when cooked. See the chapter on "Greasing without Grease," where we describe its use.

We use the granules within our recipes as an emulsifier, too, making for smoother mixtures. (And also because lecithin does such a good number on cholesterol.)

The granules should be refrigerated, but we've kept

the liquid at room temperature for months without any apparent change.

Maple Sugar

See also the next entry, "Maple Syrup."

Maple sugar is maple syrup which has been further boiled to evaporate the remaining liquid. This second boiling takes much less time than the original boiling, which turned the maple sap into maple syrup. See the recipe for *Maple Sugar* in the "Miscellany" chapter.

Any heat-sensitive vitamins which might have been in the sap were destroyed long ago in that original processing. Your current boiling to make maple sugar destroys no additional nutrients.

This is the only dry sugar we keep in the house. There are some recipes that just won't work with a liquid sweetener. We store the sugar in a covered, plastic box, where it keeps for a long, long time.

Maple Syrup

Maple syrup is the boiled-down sap of the sugar maple tree.

The tree is tapped, the sap runs into a collecting container, then, when enough is accumulated, it is run onto large boiling tables, where most of the water is boiled away, and the sweet syrup remains. The sap itself is not sweet at all and it's one of those wonders to us how it was first discovered that this nonsweet sap could be made into a sweet syrup.

Maple syrup is not quite as sweet as honey. However, it is about 15 percent lower in calories. It contains no vitamins, but it does have a surprisingly broad sampling of minerals.

Remember the difference in sweetness if you wish to substitute it in recipes calling for honey, and do note that maple syrup has a more distinctive flavor than honey does, so you don't want to use it in recipes where a flavored sweetener would be a problem.

Milk

Whole Milk

Whole liquid cow's milk contains about 3 to 4 percent complete protein (cooked soybeans are about 11 percent protein), plus several vitamins and minerals. But it certainly isn't the "wonder-food" that decades of advertising have proclaimed.

Whole milk is difficult to digest. In addition, a considerable portion of our population is allergic to milk. (See "Yoghurt," this chapter.)

As to how "whole" whole milk really is—almost all of the butterfat is removed during processing. That's right, the "whole" milk you buy has about 3.5 to 4 percent butterfat left in it, which makes those low fat milk and yoghurt claims of "98 percent fat-free" sound a little silly.

Since calcium is absorbed only in the presence of fat, we wonder how much calcium is absorbed in that 4 percent butterfat left in the milk. Perhaps the milk available in supermarkets isn't as great a source of calcium as it is touted to be.

Commercial milk is pasteurized (heated to about 145° for 30 minutes). This kills off the *tuberculosis bacillus*, but not a lot of other bacteria. The homogenization process breaks down the fat molecules even further.

We prefer raw milk which comes from certified herds. Raw milk producers must maintain high levels of sanitation and their herds and facilities are inspected frequently. Raw milk has been shown to have a lower bacteria count than pasteurized milk.

Not only is certified raw milk safe, it's neither been heated nor had its fat broken down. Butterfat content may be higher in the raw milk, too.

Skim Milk

It is our opinion, from personal experience and reading and speaking to doctors, that adults should not have whole milk. Adults who drink considerable amounts of whole milk (say, a pint or more a day) tend to be unusually susceptible to upper respiratory diseases. Adults who drink skim milk, on the other hand, are not. We have certainly proved this to our own satisfaction in our own lives.

However, bottled skim milk has a very short life in your refrigerator and it is quite expensive. Therefore, we've taken to using powdered skim milk, instant and noninstant, for both drinking and cooking.

On a glass by glass basis, the instant has been almost the same price as the noninstant, even though the latter is a health food store product and the instant is available in supermarkets.

Nutritionally, the noninstant is slightly superior. It is prepared by a low-heat process which leaves more food elements intact than you'll find in the instant. However, if something is to be cooked, we use the instant. It's easier to mix in and the advantage of the noninstant is lost in the cooking anyway.

If you're an adult and find yourself with frequent colds, by all means exchange the whole milk in your life for skim milk. However, keep the kids on whole milk; apparently they're not bothered by the butterfat as adults may be.

Supermilk

This is the word we use to describe double-strength milk.

Add twice the amount of skim milk powder as you normally would to the water. Or, add the skim milk powder to whole milk. That makes a supermilk, too.

Molasses

Molasses is the cooked liquid which remains after the crystallization of granulated sugar.

Molasses is classed much as beer is: different layers have different colors and different food values.

Light molasses is the first extraction, dark molasses is the second, blackstrap is the third. Barbados molasses comes out of a different drum.

In general, the lighter the color of the molasses, the poorer its food value. Blackstrap molasses is much superior, nutritionally, to light molasses, and much, much superior to Barbados. Blackstrap is a good source of iron, calcium, potassium, and several of the B vitamins. If you've never used it, however, start with only a little bit: the taste is strong.

Barbados molasses, which comes from the West Indies, is the only other molasses we use in this book. It contains no iron or potassium, though it does have a few of the B vitamins. Barbados is also by far the best-tasting of the lot. Barbados is generally unsulfured. Some processors add sulfur to molasses, but you don't need the sulfur they add; in fact, you're better off without it.

Nuts

Nuts are good food, especially in combination with seeds and legumes (beans). A combination like this can provide complete protein for you without ever a bit of animal protein. Nuts also contain a wide range of vitamins and minerals, a good many calories, and quite a bit of fat.

Store nuts in the shell until you're ready to eat them. They keep for a long time in the shell, but start going rancid rather quickly once shelled.

Brazil nuts will even turn rancid in the shell, so be certain you examine them and taste a few before you add them to a recipe.

Cashews should be eaten raw. It is the only nut that

is generally roasted for eating (peanuts are legumes, not real nuts). Roasting, however, destroys vitamins and enzymes. And raw cashews are quite tasty.

Pecans, as they grow on trees, have a mottled, brownish, dull shell. They get that shiny, bright shell by being bleached. Do not use bleached pecans.

Oats

We use rolled oats, both in our recipes and for oatmeal. Rolled oats come in larger pieces than steel-cut oats. To us they have a superior texture.

Oats have only moderate quality protein and a moderate range of vitamins. The major reason we use oats is for variety and for the oat flavor.

Oil

Whenever we call for oil in a recipe, we mean a liquid vegetable oil, high in polyunsaturates and cold pressed, if available—but that's just too much to write in every recipe.

Except for certain special cases, solid fats like butter are just no part of our diet. We won't talk about them here except to say that saturated, hardened fats are really only empty calories. (All liquid oils have about the same calorie count: roughly 88 calories per tablespoon.)

Cold pressing is a process whereby the seed or bean is processed in a press that doesn't generate heat. Heat destroys some vitamins. Most commercial oils are either hot pressed or obtained through a solvent process that leaves traces of the solvent in the oil.

Oils high in polyunsaturates are important to your body's proper functioning. These oils form fatty acids, which are vital to life. You cannot eliminate all oils and fats from your diet.

We use several different kinds of oils: corn oil, safflower seed oil, sunflower seed oil, and soybean oil.

We don't use coconut oil, ever, because it is too saturated. We don't use peanut oil because it is too unstable and goes rancid quickly. It is fine when fresh, however. We don't use cottonseed oil because cotton is treated and sprayed as if it were a nonfood crop, and residues get into the seed oil.

Peanuts

Peanuts are not really nuts, they are legumes. They are an even better source of protein than the true nuts.

Peanuts keep fairly well in the shell and very poorly out of the shell. Buy only nuts in the shell; shell them as you want them. Then you can be sure they're fresh.

Raw peanuts are the most nutritious, but for our palate, the flavor is too "green." You can buy raw peanuts and roast them gently in a medium oven yourself. Taste after 15 minutes or so. If they're still too raw, leave them in a little longer. We eat large amounts of peanuts all year round.

Under no circumstances buy canned shelled nuts (roasted in oil or dry roasted), or packaged salted nuts in any form—their freshness is very suspect.

Popcorn

Don't be fooled by the bad reputation popcorn has as a snack. Corn is a nutritious food, and so is popcorn, so long as you don't add a lot of unhealthy or high-calorie things to it. Don't butter it, don't salt it heavily and, most of all, don't buy it already popped and packaged.

Rice

The only difference between brown rice and white rice is that the white rice has had its nutritious outer layer ground and polished off.

However, there is a difference among various brown

rices. We use short-grain brown rice because it is cheaper than the long grain and we prefer the taste and the texture.

There is a general recipe for cooking short-grain brown rice in our "Custards" chapter.

Rice bran (or rice polish) is the ground-off coating of the rice grain. It is rich in protein and contains a broad range of vitamins and minerals in surprisingly generous amounts. The bran also contains lots of potassium and virtually no sodium. Rice bran is a little bitter, so if you're not used to eating it, start small.

Rye

Rye is a useful grain low in gluten and high in protein. The low gluten content makes rye flour difficult to knead into a bread, but the strong flavor makes it a good cracker flour or a good substitute for a little bit of whole wheat in a bread recipe (see *Bake Your Own Bread and Be Healthier*, Holt, Rinehart and Winston, 1972).

Be certain that you buy stone-ground rye flour that has not been bleached or brominated.

Salt

Salt is a poison for many people. It changes the water balance of the body's cells, makes for circulation difficulties, and causes water retention.

If your diet is high in potassium, salt is less of a problem. It seems silly to us, however, to wait for some heart specialist to put you on a low-sodium diet *after* you have a circulation problem, when you can put yourself on a low-sodium and high-potassium diet and *avoid* circulation problems.

In our recipes, we use as little salt as we can—perhaps too much or too little for your taste. But please, before you go adding salt, consider its place in your whole diet. Salt can be a real enemy.

If you use salt from the supermarket, you face another

problem: the chemicals that most salt refiners add to their products to make it free-flowing. We prefer to avoid them, so we use either sea salt (which often contains magnesium carbonate, a compound the body can use constructively), or coarse mined salt. We grind up the coarse salt ourselves. (See the "Salts" chapter in our *Blend It Splendid,* Rodale, 1973.)

If you do use sea salt or mined salt, be aware that neither contains iodine. You'll have to use some other source for your daily iodine ration (see "Kelp," this section).

Seeds

Seeds are among the best snacks you can eat. They are high in a very broad range of vitamins and contain many minerals that are difficult to come by elsewhere, such as zinc and magnesium. Sesame seeds are especially high in magnesium. Seeds even supply some amino acids missing in nuts and grains.

Sesame seeds are available both hulled and unhulled, with cortex (germ) or decorticated. We use only those with the hulls on and the germ intact. The hulls are perfectly edible (good roughage) and they keep the rather unstable sesame oil from going rancid. And the cortex holds much of the nutritive value of the seed.

Sunflower seeds we use shelled, of course. Once shelled, however, they should be stored in the refrigerator. In fact, all seeds should be refrigerated to preserve their nutrients.

Soy Flour

See "Beans" earlier in this chapter, for a rundown on soybeans.

Soy flour is available with various degrees of the fat left in: full fat, partially defatted, etc. Fat in this instance is good, not bad. It is the fat that contains the lecithin, so if you buy defatted flour you are cheating yourself of a valuable nutrient.

Soy flour has no gluten and therefore will not become elastic enough to knead into a bread on its own, at least not into a *risen* bread. It does, however, make an excellent, high-protein addition to wheat flours (see *Bake Your Own Bread and Be Healthier*, Holt, Rinehart and Winston, 1972).

Spices

See "Herbs," earlier in this chapter.

Vegetables

What can one say about vegetables that hasn't been said many times before, on both sides of the nutrition aisle?

Vegetables comprise the largest part of our diet. In this book, we've tried to use vegetables in different ways, ways that will be attractive even to confirmed vegetable haters.

Green leafy vegetables are a very important source of vitamin A, as well as vitamin C and some of the B's. Root vegetables are especially rich in minerals.

Asparagus should be eaten as soon as it is picked. Try a bit raw—you'll be surprised at the taste. If the raw asparagus doesn't taste sweet, neither will the cooked. Look at the head: if you can see flowers forming, the asparagus was probably picked too late.

The most nutritious leaves of the cabbage are the darkest outer leaves. Raw cabbage contains lots of vitamin C, which is destroyed if you cook it.

Chew carrots well. The vitamin A is otherwise "locked in" to the coarse and fibrous cellular material.

The leaves of collard greens are incredibly high in vitamin A, even higher than spinach. Their flavor is much milder. Try collards raw, in a salad.

Vinegar

Vinegar comes from the French words *vin aigre*, meaning old wine. The vinegar we use comes to us through the same fermentation process that gives us wine. Vinegar should be consumed daily in one form or another (salad dressing, pickles) because it helps maintain the acid nature of our body chemistry.

Wheat

Wheat Germ

Wheat germ is the "heart" of the wheat kernel. If you planted a wheat berry, the germ inside would sprout, feeding off the white inner part of the kernel.

This is a tremendously nutritious food, though not by any means "complete" in itself. It is rich in protein, B vitamins, potassium, and phosphorus. Wheat germ is not very stable, especially at room temperature. It must be stored in the refrigerator or the oil it contains will go rancid.

Wheat germ is available raw or toasted. Toasting serves a double purpose. It makes the bitter germ more palatable and it increases its shelf life. However, the toasting process destroys some of the food value.

Wheat Bran

Bran is the outer coating of the wheat berry, after the berry has been separated from the chaff. In milling, the germ and the bran are separated from the nutritionally inferior white (endosperm). The white goes through further grinding to become white flour, the germ is either used as animal feed or packaged for human use, and the bran is either packaged or discarded.

Bran is a very good source of B vitamins and of minerals. It is also a good roughage food for regularity.

Wheat bran, like the germ, may have a bitter taste, but the bitterness is lost when it's added to a recipe.

Bran comes in fine and coarse grinds; it doesn't really matter which you use.

Whole Wheat Flour

As the name indicates, this flour is made from the whole wheat berry, with germ, bran, and white ground together.

Whole wheat flour is not "enriched"; it doesn't need to be. Whole wheat flour has a much broader range of nutrients than does white flour, but no iron (one of the "enrichments" sometimes found in white flour). However, there is no comparing whole wheat and white flour nutritionally, either in number of nutrients or in their amounts. Whole wheat is a good food, white flour is all but a nonfood. White flour even robs the body of B vitamins.

White flour may be bleached or brominated (the flour is treated with bromine gas to increase its shelf life). Some whole wheat flour is brominated. Avoid it.

We use an organically-grown, unsprayed whole wheat flour that has been stone ground (the widely-available commercial brands are steel ground).

Whole wheat grinds vary from very fine to rather coarse. But all stone grinding is better than all steel grinding. The steel creates destructive heat that the stones do not.

Do not sift whole wheat flour. You may wind up with a sifter full of bran and a bowl containing almost-white flour.

Whole Wheat Pastry Flour

Most all-purpose whole wheat flours are made from hard wheat. Pastry flours are made from soft wheat, ground very, very fine.

This ultra-fine grinding means that little gluten can

be developed, so pastry flours are ill suited to breads. However, it is the fineness of the grind that makes them very well suited to pastry, where one would rather not come across bits of bran.

Nutritionally, pastry flour is slightly inferior to all-purpose whole wheat flour, because the soft wheat is nutritionally inferior to the hard wheat. The difference, however, is small.

Yeast, Active Dry

Active dry yeast is a living thing, or rather a colony of living things, in dormancy. Yeast requires only the addition of water and food to bring it back to active life and set it to multiplying.

Don't think that because you use only a tablespoon or two in one of our cracker or muffin recipes that you're eating only a tablespoon or two's worth of this yeast. It multiplies. By the time you eat the muffin or cracker, you've got much more yeast than you put in.

The dry form of baker's yeast is about 38 percent protein (very high) and contains a surprisingly wide range of vitamins and minerals. Keep it refrigerated.

Don't confuse active dry yeast with its near-relatives brewer's yeast or torula yeast, which are dead yeasts. These latter two are available as food supplements—excellent sources of complete protein and the B complexes.

Read your yeast's label. If your brand uses some kind of preservative in the packaging, switch brands.

Yoghurt

Yoghurt is one of the best foods because it is good on so many levels.

Yoghurt is acid. That's a plus.

Yoghurt is easy to digest.

It also provides needed bacteria to the digestive system.

Yoghurt contains many vitamins and minerals, and it is a complete protein food.

Now, that comes close to being that "perfect food" you hear the milk advertisers talking about.

Because the bacteria have "predigested" it, yoghurt can even be eaten by those who have difficulty with milk.

Keep yoghurt in the refrigerator, but eat it soon after culturing it—certainly within six days. After that, it loses a great deal of its bacterial activity, though it stays a good food on other nutritional levels for weeks.

Index